The Activist Learner

The Activist Learner

Inquiry, Literacy, and Service
to Make Learning Matter

Jeffrey D. Wilhelm
Whitney Douglas
Sara W. Fry

Foreword by
Mary Beth Tinker

Afterword by
Bruce Novak

Teachers College
Columbia University
New York and London

National Writing Project
Berkeley, CA

Published simultaneously by Teachers College Press, 1234 Amsterdam Avenue, New York, NY 10027 and National Writing Project, 2105 Bancroft Way, Berkeley, CA 94720-1042.

The National Writing Project (NWP) is a nationwide network of educators working together to improve the teaching of writing in the nation's schools and in other settings. NWP provides high-quality professional development programs to teachers in a variety of disciplines and at all levels, from early childhood through university. Through its network of nearly 200 university-based sites, NWP develops the leadership, programs and research needed for teachers to help students become successful writers and learners.

Material from "Next Steps in the Journey: Teaching with 'Urgency': A Call for Immediate Actions," from *Voices from the Middle*, 16(2), 54–57, by Jeffrey D. Wilhelm, was used throughout this work. Copyright 2008 by the National Council of Teachers of English. Reprinted with permission.

Library of Congress Cataloging-in-Publication Data can be obtained at www.loc.gov

ISBN 978-0-8077-5595-2 (paperback)
ISBN 978-0-8077-7338-3 (eBook)

Printed on acid-free paper
Manufactured in the United States of America

21 20 19 18 17 16 15 14   8 7 6 5 4 3 2 1

Contents

Foreword

Middle school students in Boise, Idaho, clamor around, excited to tell me about their school project. "See, some kids didn't have many friends, so they didn't know what to *do* during lunch," Mikey explains, waving his hands and rolling his brown eyes to show what an obvious problem this would be.

Shareese chimes in, "Now, everybody has someone to be with." The kids break into big grins, like me, as they describe the system they developed so that every student has something fun to do at lunch and a friend to do it with. I knew that the teachers who helped inspire these kids must be kindred spirits, but I didn't realize that one of them, Sara Fry, was writing this book. Soon, I would learn that the coauthors were kindred spirits as well. Jeffrey Wilhelm has "wild" ideas about kids being allowed to pursue their own reading interests. And Whitney Douglas has a special talent for getting kids excited about "inquiries."

I was in Boise as part of a year-long "Tinker Tour," a project of the Student Press Law Center, to speak with students across the country about the First Amendment, civics, students' rights, and journalism. Like the authors, I love helping students use their talents—and their rights—to make the world better. To encourage students, I tell stories of young people through history who have contributed, mostly in small ways, and often with just a little courage. In fact, I was one of them, in 1965 when I was thirteen years old and in eighth grade. That December, my father, a minister, would read us the Christmas story from the bible, with its message of hope and love. But on TV, my siblings and I watched children run from their burning huts in Vietnam, and the coffins of soldiers being sent home. My brother, John, our friend, Chris Eckhardt, and several other students had an idea. We would wear black armbands to school to "mourn the dead" and support a Christmas truce proposed by Senator Robert Kennedy. I was shy, and worried about getting in trouble. But, I had examples of people who spoke up: children in Birmingham in 1963, and adults like my parents, who had become Quakers, and took part in Mississippi Freedom Summer in 1964.

So, I decided to wear a black armband to school, with no idea that the simple action would make history. But, as I tell students, history is often made with small actions. When we were suspended, the American Civil Liberties Union filed a lawsuit. Several years later, it culminated in a landmark Supreme Court ruling that neither teachers or students "shed their Constitutional rights . . . at the schoolhouse gate" (Tinker, 1969). Subsequent Supreme Court rulings curtailed the rights of students, but the essential Tinker precedent has held. Now, I meet students all over the country who are speaking up and taking action about the many issues of their lives.

In Indiana, a high school student named Dominique tells me that she's planning to use her rights to "speak up for the oceans because oceans are amazing, and we need to protect them." She's writing an article in her school newspaper about it.

In Mississippi, Zacchaeus stands on the stage of McComb High School. We met when he and other students were honored by National History Day for creating a website and film on McComb's civil rights history. Now, students plan to start a school newspaper, and want to speak up about standardized testing, and their high school being labeled a "failing school." All over the country, and the world, young people are using their creativity, imagination, energy, and willingness to take action, as youth are inclined to do.

For others, having a voice in their schools and communities is an unknown experience, fraught with risk. They need guidance and encouragement. And, like all students, they need opportunities to participate. The ability to be heard is a skill that can be nurtured and developed.

This book is a valuable contribution to making this happen. It is part of a growing effort to make service learning an experience that goes deeper, that looks at related policies and causes of problems as well as solutions. It values not only the unique contribution of youth, but also the human rights of youth as participants in democracy.

I wish my teachers at Harding Junior High School would have had this book to guide them when I was in eighth grade. It's lucky for you and your students that you do!

Mary Beth Tinker

REFERENCE

Tinker v. Des Moines Independent Sch. Dist., 393 U.S. 503, 506 (1969).

Acknowledgments

From Jeff: Jeff wishes to send a 13-gun salute and many thanks to Sara and Whitney for their enthusiasm, vision, energy, and friendship, all applied lovingly and in manifold ways to this book project. He also wishes to give a huge thanks to his wife and partner, Peggy Jo, who inspires him in general with her courage and love in the face of her medical challenges, but who also inspires him as a teacher through her own modeling and thinking partnership. Thanks, too, to daughters Fiona and Jasmine, who have already begun a life of service to the environment and the planet through their work. A final thanks to his Boise State University colleagues who believe in and support his work, but a special thanks to Steven Olsen-Smith, Clyde Moneyhun, and Jim Fredricksen.

From Whitney: Whitney thanks coauthors Jeff and Sara for generously taking her along for the ride and invigorating her thinking, writing, and teaching in the process. She thanks Joy Ritchie, Amy Goodburn, Chris Gallagher, Debbie Minter, and Robert Brooke, whose teaching and mentoring were acts of service that forever changed who she is as a scholar and teacher. She is endlessly grateful to Jane Hill for her professional encouragement and how she made sure Whitney arrived at her destination. Big thanks to Pyper, McKenzie, and Levi—sources of unceasing support.

From Sara: Sara sincerely thanks Jeff and Whitney for their beautiful writing and their dedication to students and teachers—they are true inspirations. She also thanks her husband, Elliott, for his patience, support, and kindness. She thanks Boise State's Kara Brascia for inviting her into the world of service learning. Sara also feels profound gratitude to her parents—Pat and Bob Fry—and all the teachers she has had throughout her life who helped her learn to take action and make a difference.

***

All three of us wish to thank our editor Emily Spangler for her careful guidance on this book, Dottie Stimpson for the generous funding that supports the Boise State Writing Project service learning initiative in local schools, Gayl Loutzenhiser and Faith Beyer Hansen for their experience and expertise with service learning, and the Boise State Writing Project itself, codirector Jim Fredricksen, and all the BSWP fellows who have been involved in our inquiry and service learning courses, institutes, and implementation projects. We appreciate your service and we appreciate you!

The Activist Learner

CHAPTER 1

How Engaged and Alive We Can All Be!

Inquiry and Service for Addressing the Next Generation of Standards and Assessments

In Jeff's middle school classroom, his students work on a project to archive the stories of senior citizens, and another to provide a writing curriculum, writing groups, and thinking partners for kids residing long-term in a local cancer ward.

In Whitney's classroom, students work on projects that examine different community perspectives (health care, law enforcement, school, neighborhood) on violence in the community, creating short written pieces for a local organization's blog and newsletter.

In Sara's classroom, students examine human rights issues at global and local levels, serving with local organizations to deepen their understanding of how people collaborate to improve the human experience.

The many Boise State Writing Project teachers with whom we work as thinking partners also engage their students in service learning as part of their regular curriculum and their quest to meet the next generation of standards. High school teacher Jerry Hendershot's students work with local artists to promote community art to highlight and celebrate Idaho's heritage. Middle school teacher Nikki Jones's students serve as homework mentors and peer editors at a writing center. Middle school teacher Yoli Gonzalez extends a civil rights unit into a schoolwide and then communitywide antibullying project. Elementary teacher Trish Mizuta's students pursue a project promoting responsible and compassionate pet ownership. And this is just the tip of the proverbial iceberg.

We teach in a world that is stunningly beautiful and filled with possibility, populated by diverse peoples, environments, cultures, and geography. At the same time, we teach in a world that is overwhelmingly complex with its issues of discrimination, poverty, disease, and environmental destruction. Filled with some of the young inhabitants of this world, our classrooms hold empowering potential for teaching students generative ways to think and actively apply their learning to work toward substantive change rather than feeling overwhelmed and powerless.

Recognizing our students as innovative agents of change makes teaching an act of empowerment and love, not only toward our students but also toward the people and environments outside our classrooms. We as teachers are simultaneously empowered by the knowledge that our students are activist learners in a world that needs them to assume a dynamic, agentive, activist mindset.

ANGELA'S FRIENDSHIP AND CITIZENSHIP UNIT

An inspiring story of students as activist learners took place in Boise State Writing Project (BSWP) fellow Angela Housley's classroom when she found herself with a very diverse group of 4th-grade students. The group featured different levels of academic achievement, of socio-economic status (SES); a wide variety of social, emotional and intellectual needs; and a boy with Asperger's. One of the first things Angela noticed was that she could not, in all good conscience, live with the exclusion and rejection that was apparent inside her classroom and outside on the playground. She decided to address the issue in a variety of implicit, "come through the back door" kinds of ways, and also with explicit "through the front door, let's inquire into this together" methods.

Angela had been engaged for several years in inquiry-oriented teaching that included various levels and categories of service learning. Angela regularly began her school year with a unit framed around the question "What makes a good friend and citizen?" She intentionally framed this issue that students already care about—friendship—as an "existential" question (Wilhelm & Novak, 2011) to explore, as a life problem to be addressed together and perhaps even solved.

In this unit, students read a wide variety of texts, comparing and contrasting different characters and historical figures; composing different kinds of narratives, informational texts, and arguments; and also creating trading cards citing their classmates' strengths as superheroes. Angela layered a new level onto the inquiry with the subquestion, "How can we be good friends and citizens on the playground to make the best possible playground experience for everyone?"

Angela's class enthusiastically engaged in conflict resolution, the creation of new playground rules, and also composed a playground user's guide that provided pointers for inclusion. The 4th-graders also developed new, inclusive games of their own invention and modified rules for existing games to promote maximum enjoyment and inclusion, both at school and at home.

The students engaged not only in inquiry-based learning, but also in the application of what they had learned in personal and classroom settings. They did so with the utmost enthusiasm and seriousness, navigating many significant challenges in wide-awake ways.

One group of boys modified their football games to include Willie, the boy with Asperger's. Throughout the game, Willie was allowed to be on either team and to play any role he liked that did not involve handling the ball (because he did not fully understand the rules of football). After every touchdown, the first kickoff went to Willie, who was allowed to catch the ball and run among all the other players and score a touchdown. Then he celebrated with everyone, after which there was a new kickoff and the game proceeded. Willie was provided with what Lave and Wenger (1991) call "legitimate peripheral participation"—that is, he was allowed to participate at the level of his capacity, to be part of the game, and if the opportunities arose, his participation was made fuller and more legitimate.

One day, a new boy entered the class. That day during recess, he rejected the rules of the modified football game. When the children reentered their classroom, they demanded a "class meeting," a ritual for negotiating problems and reflecting on the group's work together. Angela initiates the class meeting process in the early weeks of school, and the children quickly take ownership of the process. A video camera was running, and the sequence of events is riveting and moving to watch.

The boys explained that the new student did not "understand how we play football to include Willie." Willie—who, like many individuals with Asperger's, rarely spoke—asked if he could speak. Everyone quieted. He stood and explained how he had been included and how this made him part of the group, but that the new boy wanted to change the rules back to what they used to be, which would mean that Willie would have to sit on the sidelines.

The glistening faces of the students on the tape, damp with tears of uplift and joy, the way Willie spoke for himself and others supported him, the commitment of the group to inclusion—something that had been cultivated over time and through great challenges—and the growing understanding and induction of the new boy into this new kind of classroom culture are powerful reminders of the effects of meaningful educational experiences that involve some kind of service to the self and to others.

Angela has found that students like Willie, who normally struggle to "play school well," thrive with service learning. She joyfully commented, "Service learning provides a place for everyone—and ways for everyone to make places for others and find places of their own."

This is the kind of service we will promote in this book: service that deepens, enriches, and applies the work of the curriculum; that abets the engagement and learning of reading, composing, speaking and listening, language, deep conceptual and strategic development and understanding; but also leads us into the world in ways that make us better people while fulfilling the larger purposes of education that should always be front and center.

SERVICE LEARNING DEFINED

Service learning is frequently misconceived as big extracurricular projects, conflated with community service hours or volunteerism. In contrast, we embrace a practical approach to service learning, where curricular goals are integrated with the lived reality of students and result in some form of helpful activity and application—active assistance that we could call service—to the self, to others, and to some form of community, whether this community be the classroom; school; a locality; a disciplinary, regional, or global community; or even the environment.

We argue that the service learning process should result in some kind of contribution to ongoing disciplinary and real-world conversations and activity about how to make meaning, apply learning, and be in the world. In other words, the learning process is a loop that results in service to the self and others as well as some kind of service to the discipline being studied and to the work of that discipline in real-world application. We claim that the instructional model best suited to deep understanding and use, for meeting the next generation of standards and assessments, and for most naturally and coherently integrating service is "inquiry," defined as the rigorous apprenticeship into disciplinary expertise and application.

INQUIRY AND ITS IMPORTANCE TO SERVICE

Inquiry is an instructional model that situates learning in lived experience, connects this experience to the curriculum, and guides students to address real-world issues in a consciously crafted classroom culture. Inquiry-based teaching focuses on guiding students to address a real-life problem, and perhaps even solve it in some way or to some degree. Instruction is based on an existential question (Wilhelm & Novak, 2011). Existential questions frame the curricular topic as a personally compelling problem to be solved and pique student interest while addressing disciplinary understandings and strategies like those required in the Common Core State Standards (CCSS). These questions also reward and require various levels of service. Simply put, existential questions focus on *how* to *be* in the world, and how to *act* in the world (Wilhelm & Novak, 2011).

Newman and colleagues (1995, 1996) provided gold-standard studies supporting inquiry as the most powerful teaching model for facilitating students' deep understanding and application of what is learned. Inquiry units are easy to justify under the new CCSS and other next generation standards, as inquiry is clearly the best way to enliven and meet those standards. The standards are all procedural (versus content oriented) and involve wide reading and writing, analysis, inference-making, seeing from multiple perspectives, short and extended research projects, and the strategies of representing, sharing, justifying, and applying what has been learned; all of these actions are required in inquiry environments (Hillocks, 1983, 1995; Newman & Associates, 1996; Newman & Wehlage, 1995; Wilhelm, 2007). Another power of inquiry is that it requires students to connect personally and compellingly with the curricular material, and in turn connect and apply their learning back to the real world (Wilhelm, 2007).

Service applies what is learned through inquiry in ways that matter—to students, to others near and far, and to the world in which students live. If teachers and students cannot identify culminating compositions, social actions, and service learning projects that apply what has been learned to real-world activity, then they are not pursuing genuine inquiry. Integrating service learning into the curriculum therefore requires a movement toward inquiry and the strategies of meaning-construction required by the new standards.

As Angela says, "Service learning is a test case for good curriculum and instruction. When you put learning to use in service of the self or others, you are demonstrating understanding and application and the absolute importance and usefulness of what's been learned." The takeaway: All inquiry results in some kind of service to self and to others.

EFFECTIVE SERVICE LEARNING

In our own work promoting service learning in classrooms and schools, we have found that service works best when it is:

1. integrated into the curriculum as part and parcel of the ongoing educational process in the classroom, focusing the class on personal and social applications of what is being learned in terms of disciplinary knowledge;
2. fitted to be central and complementary to preexisting learning goals rather than being something extra;
3. connected to students, and to their learning substantive, challenging content and strategies that intersect with their lived experiences;
4. framed to make the learning process naturally engaging, applicable both immediately and in the future; and
5. framed to consciously cultivate joy, love, caring, the creation of constructive possibilities for the self and others now and in the future, and most important, the cultivation of wisdom in the stances, attitudes, and actions of teacher and students (Wilhelm & Novak, 2011).

We are obviously angling after big fish here, and we have invoked the word *wisdom*. We have done so purposefully. One of our central arguments is that teaching, though it must be substantive in terms of learning content and strategies, must address the next generation of standards like the CCSS and must prepare students for new assessments and success in college and career and *also needs to be something more*. The best teaching—the kind of teaching that keeps teachers passionate and engaged year after year (Nieto, 2003), that deeply engages students, leads to the deepest understanding and application of knowledge, and transforms students while preparing them for futures not just as workers and learners but as democratic citizens and compassionate human beings—is profoundly informed by higher purposes such as love and wisdom (Wilhelm & Novak, 2011).

Our pedagogical goals must involve making lasting, transformative differences, as students learn that caring, generosity, and service are important ways of knowing and making meaning in the academic world as well as the world outside of school. We believe wholeheartedly that teachers and students must work together in wide-awake ways toward ongoing service, joy, love, and wisdom.

In Jeff and Bruce Novak's book on wisdom (Wilhelm & Novak, 2011), wisdom was defined as:

> [B]ecoming increasingly more conscious of interconnectedness (between people, between groups, and between people and creation); developing a profound respect for others and other perspectives; cultivating caring and compassion; being guided by a greater good than materialism, status and image; valuing stillness and reflection—and seeking guidance from an inner versus outer locus of control; developing inner awareness of one's own identity, perceptions, motivation and possibilities; and a commitment to application and agency: to service and social action for a communitarian good. (pp. 202–203)

Service is central to our definition of wisdom; we believe that all aspects of wisdom necessarily culminate in service to the self and for communitarian good. Service can be integrated and performed on multiple levels, and different types of service make it possible for teachers to more readily integrate service in ways that closely align with curricular goals.

Levels and Categories of Service

There are many levels and categories of service, and we have found that a prerequisite to mindful engagement in any service is that students must cultivate attitudes, internalize concepts, and master procedures that allow them, as sociocultural theorists and cognitive scientists would say, to "self-regulate." When self-regulating, students strive to consciously solve problems and reflectively monitor their own strategic activity and behavior.

The internal reflectiveness that self-regulation makes possible is necessary to all deep learning, and is prerequisite to other levels of service, such as assisting peers, small groups, the classroom, the school, and local and global communities in collective moves toward heightened awareness and consciousness. Service to others can then lead to creating more assistive and productive structures, inspiring more kindness and compassion, and adopting wiser attitudes and activities. Self-regulation and growth in understanding are also essential for contributing to disciplinary conversations, even as novices, and for contributing to the creation of evolving disciplinary and real-world cultures.

Within levels of service, there are different categories of service. Kaye (2010) provided a nice summary when she discussed:

1. Direct service: providing direct assistance to the self or others, usually in a personal, face-to-face way that typically requires involvement over time, from the beginning to the end of some kind of project. Examples of direct service are cleaning up a lake, serving a meal in a homeless shelter, or reading to vision-impaired residents in a nursing facility.
2. Indirect service: providing assistance from a distance. Examples of indirect service are peer advice and letter-writing buddies, taking calls on a peer hotline, or conducting and contributing archival research to a larger community project.
3. Advocacy: creating heightened awareness or promoting action on the part of others. Advocacy typically involves secondary research that is shared with others; examples include maintaining a social action website, contributing to newsletters, creating public service announcements (PSAs), organizing and participating in a town meeting, or running a book club.
4. Research: engaging in critical inquiries (typically extending topical inquiries from the classroom; Wilhelm, 2007) where students conduct primary research through interviews, surveys, frame experiments, and evaluations that are then shared with peers, community members, or even with the discipline in journals or websites devoted to student research.

Inquiry should always result in some kind of service to self and to peers, and some kind of direct service. Many inquiry units involve various levels of service and all categories of service. The service we value (1) guides students to see how the world around them, wherever they are, is a source of inquiry and (2) helps students identify how they can participate in important conversations and social projects in multiple current and future contexts.

Moving Toward Principled Practices

Service learning can help meet current needs at the school, community, and global levels brought on by various constraints as well as newly arising and highly complex challenges. However, few schools assist teachers to support students in doing this kind of work or to integrate service learning into the curriculum in ways that motivate and promote student growth as strategic thinkers and content-area learners. That is the challenge we have been undertaking with our service learning initiative, and that we report on in this book.

We are grateful to previous work on service learning in K–12 contexts. Some of the niches we aim to help fill in this work are to provide principles of practice, a theory of practice and application geared toward transfer, and concrete models that exemplify this principled practice.

Seven central principles of practice underpin the approach to inquiry and service learning that we advocate:

1. Service learning should function "in service" to deep conceptual and strategic learning and should be the result of newly developed and deep understandings.
2. Service focuses our attention on higher purposes for learning. Beyond the standards we teach for in literacy, problem-solving, strategic, and conceptual understanding, there are higher purposes and goals that enliven our teaching, engage our students, and lead us all toward love and wisdom. These purposes include teaching for environmental stewardship, for civic engagement, for compassion, and much more.
3. Service is best combined with inquiry models of teaching. Inquiry requires and rewards the essential measure of understanding through application; service is a critical element of that application. Inquiry is also the model for meeting the next generation of standards and assessments such as the CCSS and commensurate standards in the United States (e.g., Smith, Appleman, & Wilhelm, 2014; Wilhelm & Novak, 2011).
4. Service has many layers: service to the self, peers, small groups, classroom or local community, global communities, and the environment. All classroom learning should contribute to the first three layers, and we can often extend this learning and service to other layers.
5. Service can and should be naturally integrated into classroom learning projects, engaging students in disciplinary conversations and applications in ways that serve those conversations and make knowledge usable.
6. Service is an attitude and stance that we cultivate on a daily level in the classroom and in our lives that connects us more deeply and reciprocally to our selves, to others, and to the world.
7. Service should help youth build the skills and the interest to become adults who actively participate in a democracy and endeavor to improve society (Allen, 2003; Kahne & Middaugh, 2008).

These seven principles are at the heart of our teaching, shaping our identities and attitudes as teachers, curricular planning and implementation, relationships with our students, and the classroom cultures that we consciously strive to create.

CREATING CLASSROOM CULTURES OF INQUIRY AND SERVICE

To prepare students for success (versus reacting to deficits), teachers must frame clear and compelling purposes for learning and shape contexts that require and reward particular kinds of learning that we value and specify. Contextualizing instruction is what cognitive scientists have named *situated cognition* (Brown,

Collins, & Duguid, 1989) and what Hillocks (1983, 1995) called *environmental teaching*. Situated cognition is about creating cultures that coproduce and require specific kinds of learning and its application.

Creating meaningful classroom cultures through inquiry that leads to action (including service) is a powerful and well-known idea in educational research and cognitive science (see, e.g., Newman & Associates, 1996; Newman & Wehlage, 1995; Smith & Wilhelm, 2002, 2006). Everything from vocabulary growth to deep strategic and conceptual understandings (such as those required by the CCSS and the next generation of standards and assessments worldwide) is best achieved when students understand the purpose and the immediate possibilities for applying what is learned in authentic, actual contexts.

Angela's purposeful construction of an inclusive classroom culture that values all students and allows her students to develop meaningful goals as outlined in the CCSS is one example of how teachers can achieve these skills. We'll explore Angela's approach in more depth in subsequent chapters as we further identify how her students develop skills that are important for a lifetime, not just 4th grade.

Focusing on an immediate and pressing classroom concern can lead to learning that lasts, as Vivian Gussin Paley's (1993) beautiful book *You Can't Say You Can't Play* illustrates. Set in her kindergarten classroom late in her career, the book focuses on how Paley became increasingly troubled by how her students excluded one another—at what she called "the habit of rejection"—and even more troubled at how she had been aware of the problem throughout her career and had never directly taken it on.

She decided to do so, head on, in hopes that addressing this problem would be of service to herself, her teaching, the classroom, her students, and their as yet unlived possibilities and futures—and eventually to their future academic and social lives and to the larger community and world.

Addressing the issue indirectly and through the "back door," she wrote stories about the adventures of the fictional Magpie, who dealt with friendship, acceptance, and rejection. She shared the stories with the children, and they illustrated them, acted them out, and often used them to inspire their own storytelling.

The direct, "front door" process began when a student named Clara was rejected, went crying into her cubby, and wouldn't come out. Paley (1993) recognized the issue she had avoided over her years of teaching and decided to take action. Calling her students together, she discussed Clara's sadness at being made to feel unwanted, and told the students that she could not get the following question out of her mind: "Is it fair for children in school to keep another child out of play? After all, the classroom belongs to all of us" (Paley, 1993, pp. 13–16).

Paley (1993) then proposed a rule: "You can't say you can't play." The socially successful students resisted the rule more directly. Students who self-identified as outsiders liked the rule and the fairness of it, but even they were mostly dubious that it would work.

Implementation of "the rule," as Paley's students referred to it, offered many challenges as well as opportunities for discussion and reflection, especially an examination of a variety of behaviors that demonstrated the new rule's effectiveness. Most important, the students internalized new ways of being, acting, thinking, valuing, speaking for themselves and others, productively monitoring themselves and others, including and assisting one another, and creating a more open and transformative classroom culture.

When she was interviewed about her study in an episode of NPR's *This American Life* on the cruelty of children, Paley (Glass, 1996) related a story about Lisa, the student who most resisted the idea and implementation of "the rule." Five years after Lisa's kindergarten year, Paley encountered Lisa and her mother in the grocery store. Lisa greeted Paley and asked, "How is the rule doing?" Paley told her that the rule was doing well, though many students found it hard to follow. Lisa said, "I try to follow the rule every day. But it's still hard for me, too." Lisa's mother told Paley, "She really does try, you know."

We love this moving story of a teacher creating a classroom environment that leverages, encourages, requires, and rewards various levels of service: the service of self-regulation, service to others and the community, service to the present moment and to the future. The internalization and valuing of other perspectives and the commitment to inclusion and the community that Paley (1993) illuminated does not happen by accident but must be actively cultivated.

Inquiry and service function as critical acts of intervention when students position themselves in new agentive ways and participate purposefully both in and beyond the classroom. Paley (1993) and Angela's approaches that guide students to deep learning through service are supported by cognitive science research.

COGNITIVE SCIENCE AND PURPOSEFUL LEARNING

If we think in terms of learning as necessarily functioning in service to the self, peers, and community, then our instruction shifts toward the sociocultural practices supported by current cognitive science (Rogoff, Matusov, & White 1996; Wilhelm, Baker, & Dube, 2001). These sociocultural theories and practices undergird the next generation of standards and assessments with their focus on higher-order thinking, and the actual performance of reading, composing, speaking, and listening in order to accomplish disciplinary work.

Such an emphasis on application incorporates various levels of service and helps us focus on using the *why* and *how* to get after the *what*, instead of the focus on inert information that has so long dominated American education (Wilhelm, Baker, & Dube, 2001).

Contemporary work in the cognitive sciences and brain research on neuroplasticity support a focus on service learning. Some of the relevant points from this research include:

- The mind can be trained to change the brain; activities and habits create neurological pathways in the brain that make these activities and habits more accessible.
- Neurons and neuronal networks grow throughout the course of a lifetime based on experiences and activities, and the growth comes from working through new challenges in meaningful contexts with focused support and practice.
- Nurture is more powerful than nature when it comes to brain structuring and ways of thinking, behaving, and being.
- People can overcome negative prior experiences, habits, and ways of being, strokes, and severe brain injuries with the right environments and support—and this process actually reconfigures the physical structure of the brain (see, e.g., Doidge, 2007).

Inquiry and service learning create an environment that stimulates and reinforces the habits and growth of mind necessary for lifelong learning and taking ethical stances and actions in the world.

Research in epigenetics (Shenk, 2010) has demonstrated that we can shape the world as much as the world shapes us, and that everything we do—every stance, attitude, and strategy we employ—not only changes our brain but can also affect our own future behavior and the expression of our genes. Epigenetics has shown that cultivated attitudes and ways of being can be passed down genetically through the epigenome. Our habits of activity and attitude change not only our brains but our genes—and therefore our future propensities and the lives of others.

This kind of research, though still in its infancy, indicates that there are profound possibilities in educating for transformation and service. Teaching through inquiry and service, then, is about creating classroom cultures that foster the best in all students—not only intellectually but also emotionally, psychically, physically, and transpersonally (Wilhelm & Smith, 2014)—and as teachers we are educating the whole person toward ongoing innovation and transformation in social situations and cultures both in and beyond the classroom.

THE EMPOWERING NOTION OF THIRD SPACE

When we discuss a new kind of classroom culture, we are referring to the creation of what has often been called a "third space"—a transformational space that is neither the culture of the home nor of traditional school, but a transitional space that melds the cultural capital of both in ways that are not constrained by either (Moje et al., 2004). The famed psychologist D. W. Winnicott (1953) indicated that a "third space" exists *between* the "subjective" and the "objective." An inherent site of possibility, third space guides students to productively travel in new worlds: those of others and of other communities and disciplines.

Applied to teaching and learning processes, third space:

- requires the integration of home and school funds of knowledge;
- provides democratic spaces where new meanings
  and ways of being can be created;
- is a place of cogenerative dialogue among all interested and
  affected parties—inside and outside the classroom;
- draws on students' out-of-school interests and home resources
  and literacies in ways that can be fused with schooled literacy and
  disciplinary knowledge. This process can proceed in transformative
  ways that are applicable in school and home and beyond; and
- involves deep connection to problems and to those
  engaged with and affected by those problems.

Inquiry combined with service learning creates a third space wherein students develop new knowledge and ways of being through deep connections to problems and to others. This connectedness has lasting benefits; as Rachel Kessler (2000) explained, connected students thrive because "[t]hey feel they belong—that people know them. Suffering and violence trail the lives of those who are without such connections. Students who thrive have had parents or teachers who have provided a wealth of opportunities for deep connection" (p. 19).

We have repeatedly seen how students thrive in third spaces such as Angela Housley's classroom, and we believe in the ongoing possibilities that inquiry and service learning hold for shaping third spaces.

GENERAL APPROACH AND JUSTIFICATION

In this book, we demonstrate how an inquiry model of teaching that rigorously apprentices students into disciplinary and real-world expertise naturally includes and is enriched by a service learning pedagogy. Both inquiry and service learning cultivate, require, and reward literacy as well as democracy. Through service learning projects, students develop and apply literacy and disciplinary knowledge, see firsthand the real-world implications and uses of their learning, learn to think in more connected ways, and simultaneously acquire literacies that are essential for sustaining a culture of democratic collaboration and civic engagement.

The emphasis on inquiry, associated with deep understanding and use, is timely in this era of the next generation of standards and assessments. The emphasis on service is also timely. Many schools across the country are requiring senior projects that often have a service component or are requiring service learning as a graduation requirement. Multiple colleges and universities have revised their core general education requirements, incorporating at least one or more core courses and/or institutionwide learning outcomes that focus on ethical thinking and civic engagement.

We three authors—Jeff, Whitney, and Sara—have all been longtime proponents of inquiry-oriented learning environments to situate student learning of literacy and the achievement of deep understanding (e.g., Smith, Appleman, & Wilhelm, 2014; Wilhelm, 2007; Wilhelm & Novak, 2011; Wilhelm, Wilhelm, & Boas, 2008). In inquiry-oriented learning, we have argued for framing the curricular topic as an existential question, a compelling problem to be solved with personal and social consequences in the real world. Our approach rigorously apprentices students into deeper disciplinary expertise, conceptually and strategically, while developing their capacities to be in the world and to apply what they have learned in socially responsible and communitarian ways.

Along these lines, we've endeavored to create situations where students apply what they have learned during their inquiries through various kinds of compositions and culminating projects, including some form of social action or service. We've all engaged in teaching, both on our own and in collaboration with others, that integrates service learning into our curriculum and instruction in ways that help to powerfully meet curricular goals and standards such as the CCSS.

The three of us have also worked together through a service learning initiative sponsored by the Boise State Writing Project that has led to the development of engaging inquiry-oriented curriculum from grades K to 12 (and even at the college level) wherein more than 100 teachers over the past few years have developed and implemented a variety of service learning projects.

In subsequent chapters, we will share our stories and methods for reframing existing curricula into an inquiry-based approach that integrates service learning and social action. We will also show how our approach meets the next generation of standards (e.g., the CCSS), prepares K–12 students for the next generation of assessments, and situates students for problem solving in life and democratic citizenship.

In each chapter, we examine a different category of service, offering rich portraits of integrated service learning projects in the context of inquiry. Through our examination, we show how to provide meaningful situations for applying and using knowledge, suggest practical guidelines for using service learning to meet the next generation of standards/assessments, and promote a form of activist literacy that works for the self, others, and the community.

We include real-world portraits to model how teachers can naturally integrate service learning into the curriculum in ways that do not create extra work and instead assist with the work that all teachers and students must do. The portraits also make visible some of the common challenges that teachers face with service learning, demonstrating how challenges can be negotiated and ultimately are not deterrents to integrating service learning but are, in fact, opportunities for deep learning and reflection. We also highlight daily activities and smaller-scale projects that demonstrate the feasibility of adopting a service learning approach whether or not it leads to larger or long-term projects.

Our main message: All teachers at any level can use service learning to inspire and engage students in the context of the regular classroom curricula and projects; teachers do not require parent volunteers or an office of service learning in order to transform their classrooms into spaces where students make purposeful and intentional service one of the products of their learning. We believe that from an early age students can develop the vital habits of mind that are necessary for active and ethical participation in a democratic society, and they do so in ways that will motivate, enliven, and deepen their learning.

In order to act on our beliefs about students, we ask the following existential questions of ourselves as teachers. These questions underpin this book:

- How can we leverage the unique potential of the classroom community to do what can only be done when we are working together on significant projects?
- What are our bottom lines as teachers? What are the absolutely essential goals that we want to meet with students? What are the achievements that we feel we must reach? What would make us feel that we had not fully actualized students' potential in a particular course or year?
- What keeps us going as teachers? What are the goals and purposes that keep teachers inspired through the inevitable challenges and difficulties? What is the prize, and how do we keep our eyes on that prize? (See Nieto, 2003.)
- What are the larger cultural projects and stories that we want to contribute to and that we want our students to participate in as individuals and together?

To supplement the text throughout the chapters, the reader is directed to a special feature of this book, an online appendix of figures. They are indicated by the format "see **Online Figure**" followed by a letter. This additional information can be accessed on the Teachers College Press website (http://tcpress.com) under Free Downloads.

LOOKING TOWARD TRANSFORMED FUTURES

We have learned that hardness in terms of rigor and softness in terms of compassion and service are in no way mutually exclusive. In fact, they are symbiotic processes. We can be both rigorous—or, perhaps even better, vigorous—and soft at the same time.

One of the tragedies of much educational experience is how easily it could be different. The next generation of standards can be leveraged toward deeper engagement and transformative teaching; this can be done even under great constraints, with just a few changes to what we already do. With some simple reframing (of curriculum into inquiry, of teaching for engaged transaction instead of information transmission), we can meet our students' basic human needs for motivation, accomplishment, community, and much more. This is one of the implicit possibilities of our current historical moment and the next generation of standards and assessments. The question remains: How will we implement such standards, and how will we choose to actualize the possibilities of our own teaching and our students' learning?

CHAPTER 2

Existential Inquiry

The Process of Integrating Service Learning into the Curriculum

In this chapter, we will discuss the practical considerations related to planning inquiry units that achieve our biggest goals for students, including deep conceptual understandings and new strategic capacities (such as those featured in the next generation of standards like the CCSS Anchor Standards and associated assessments) that are applied not only to academic work and culminating compositions and projects but also to students' lived experience—and as forms of service to the self, others, and community.

ASKING EXISTENTIAL QUESTIONS

Jeff's wife, Peggy Jo, is a highly accomplished teacher. Several years ago, she collapsed with what turned out to be a life-threatening and as yet unnamed disease. Peggy Jo has courageously and gracefully dealt with her condition in very inspiring ways. Being engaged in such a struggle, among other things, has steeled her attention to what is most important.

A few years ago, in the midst of this health struggle, Jeff was planning yet another iteration of a *Romeo and Juliet* unit, which he has taught many times. Peggy Jo directly challenged Jeff: "How are you teaching for wisdom and use, for understanding and service, in the context of this unit?"

Jeff argued that the inquiry question "What makes a good relationship?" would encourage his students to reflect on relationships and engage in healthier relationships. Peggy Jo thought he was being facile. "You are assuming a lot!" she said.

She pushed Jeff. He kept revising his question to make it an existential question by placing it inside students' lived experiences and directly challenging them to learn and apply something of service to their own existence and that of others: "What makes and breaks relationships, and what can we do to foster healthier relationships for ourselves and others?"

Peggy Jo kept pushing: How are you helping the kids learn how to be respectful of themselves and others? How are you helping them to practice this in the unit? How are you helping students: to reframe relational issues in positive ways, to reframe problems into possibilities, and complaints into commitments? to relate to others with compassion and kindness? to care for the absolute personhood of their partners? to enter into and value other perspectives? to think about where to draw the line when a relationship is not mutually healthy or respectful?

When Jeff acknowledged that he wasn't exactly sure if he would be getting after these issues directly, Peggy Jo asked, "Then what are you teaching for?"

She emphasized: "You better make literature and writing and all curriculum about *life and living.*"

Just as authors benefit from editors who help them craft the best writing possible, teachers benefit from thinking partners who push them to design the best learning experiences possible. Through her astute questions, Peggy Jo pushed Jeff beyond his usual practice and toward existential questions in the context of inquiry-based teaching. Her challenge to Jeff guided him to create a more compelling and purposeful unit for his students.

Refining the existential question to get at what really matters—what we should be teaching for—is critical. By considering broad questions such as those Peggy Jo posed, we move toward situating class activities and assignments in conversation with students' lives and experiences, thus creating a third space wherein greater teaching and learning possibilities lie.

AN INQUIRY UNIT ON VOICE

Jeff and his colleague and thinking partner Sarah Veigel each taught versions of a unit on voice that enacted all aspects of inquiry and incorporated service learning. Their unit versions are excellent examples of how the framework for one high school English language arts unit can be implemented and retooled as an existential inquiry for an effective learning experience in multiple contexts.

Jeff's unit was framed with the existential question: Whose story gets told? The subquestions included: Why do certain stories get told? Whose stories get silenced and why? What are the results of certain stories being told and certain stories being silenced? How can we elicit silenced or hidden stories? How can we become good listeners?

Sarah taught 9th-graders a more personalized version of the unit that prompted students to reflect on themselves, moving outward to explore how both self and others could be listened to. Sarah framed her unit with the existential question: Who am I (and who are we), and how can I (we) be heard?

Jeff believes that all learning must involve some kind of service to the self that creates some kind of lasting change in the student in practical, reflective, and metacognitive terms. Learning, as a service to the self, should help students rehearse for future applications and ways of being, for navigating and solving problems, and for getting work done. This is part of his attraction to inquiry: It naturally leads to deep understanding, transfer, and use. Sarah has likewise always been dedicated to learning that results in reaching out to others and the community, and to applications of learning that do work for the self and out in the world.

In every story or informational text that they read in these units, the students engaged in recursive learning as they asked: Whose story is being told and why? How is the story positioning the characters and us as the audience? What is the story being told for/against? Whose story is not being told and why? How can we elicit or imagine the silenced voices (through drama, imagination, research, and so on)?

For the culminating unit activity, Jeff's students engaged in two storytelling projects. First, they made videotaped micronarratives of unheard stories. These stories could come from their own perspectives or the perspective of another person whom they had interviewed. The stories were either about a positive experience and outcome, a struggle resulting in a positive outcome, or a struggle that could be addressed in a way that helped others identify insights about overcoming challenges. In the second project, all students interviewed senior citizens about their lives, asking the senior citizens to tell stories that they may not have told for some time, and what advice they would give to younger people such as themselves.

Students then composed multimedia narratives and counternarratives (e.g., the mainstream cultural story about World War II, Vietnam, and immigration juxtaposed with the personal, often mainstream-resistant and marginalized stories), compiled their stories in a community storybook, and created a multimedia exhibit at the local history museum organized around the theme of "Our Community's Stories."

Although the focus throughout the unit was on service to self (learning to skillfully converse, broach topics, deal with difficult subjects, interview and listen to others, and to unsilence the self), the unit also led the class to provide service to the community. Jeff's students helped people with silenced, unheard stories to tell their stories in ways that were of service to themselves and the community, and created archival knowledge artifacts for the future.

In Sarah's class, students wrote problem/solution papers about a problem involving silenced or unheard stories. Boise is one of the great refugee cities of North America, and there are more than 200 different languages spoken in our schools. Almost all the refugee students at Sarah's school had escaped political oppression and danger to their lives by leaving their homeland and coming to the United States. Many of them had been in refugee camps and had limited formal schooling. Following their problem/solution paper assignment, Sarah's students wrote calls to action that shaped specific service learning activities to address the problems—such as helping refugee classmates in Boise find transportation or ways to interact with the school community through an intramural program, communal lunch banquets, buddy and mentoring programs, and the like. The presence of refugee populations in our Boise community reinforces the value of a service learning approach that addresses the real needs of students and others in theoretically sound and mindful ways while also creating transformative learning experiences.

Tony, one of Jeff's students, had this to say at the end of the unit: "In a lot of ways I totally changed my mind [about the Vietnam War], but in other ways I feel even more strongly the way I did [at the start of the unit] but that's funny because these feelings kinda got stronger by seeing other ways of seeing—by seeing that I have a way of thinking that is like some people and different from some other people." His classmate Lacey commented, "I felt like I learned to listen to others and to really try to hear them and value what they were saying—other people but characters, too, but maybe even more, I learned to listen to myself and hear myself in new ways. That was really kind of tight and fun and empowering."

At the end of the units on voice, students reflected on what they had learned and how to transfer this learning to their futures, generating ideas for how to listen to themselves in the face of obstacles, how to talk to others, elicit stories, value multiple perspectives, be good listeners, create situations and events for sharing stories, and create community. Learning outcomes from Sarah's and Jeff's units illustrate how meaningful service inspires students and (re)positions them in more democratically minded ways in the world by cultivating valuable personal, social, and academic skills and dispositions.

STARTING OFF: ARTICULATING OUR LARGEST GOALS

A central premise of this book is that in an age of next generation of standards and assessments that can seem inspiring, unwieldy, and/or unpredictable and that will obviously focus much of our work as teachers, we still need to (and can!) keep our eyes on the prize of larger goals. We believe that our teaching is most passionate, our students' learning is most engaged, and the standards are best met when we teach in contexts of meaningful use, in service of our most cherished bottom lines, not only as teachers but as human beings. We further believe, to quote Angela Housley: "Service learning is *the best* and most powerful *stimulus* and culmination of units that meet the next generation standards and assessments."

To get after these bottom lines, we use an activity with teachers in our service learning initiative that we call the "bottom lines" activity (Wilhelm, Baker, & Dube, 2001). We ask teachers to articulate their absolute bottom lines for their teaching (see Figure 2.1). What is it that they absolutely must achieve with their students during their time together—or they would feel that their most important purposes and missions as a teacher had not been fulfilled?

Answers about bottom lines are big, and they serve as potent reminders of what brought us into teaching and what keeps teaching immensely significant and satisfying work for us. They remind us of how to keep our classroom "toolish" in terms of both functional work and "inner work" (Wilhelm & Smith, 2014) instead of merely "schoolish" (Smith & Wilhelm, 2002, 2006); how to help students experience the kind of joy we savor when we learn in ways that enrich ourselves and others; and how to foster learning that serves practical, real-world purposes.

Figure 2.1. Thinking Big: Reaching Toward Our Bottom Lines

- What is absolutely most important to know and to be able to do to be a whole and fulfilled human being?
- How are schools, assessments, policies, and the like serving these purposes? Or not?
- What are the transformational possibilities of literacy education and education in general?
- What can we do as teachers to work for higher purposes within current constraints? How can we leverage the next generation of standards and assessments for progressive transformations that will help us meet our bottom lines?
- How can I help my students progress toward bottom line goals in my classroom?

Initial answers from our teachers are general. Bottom lines may be grounded in considerations of the *emotional*—for example, helping every child feel safe and accepted. *Political* bottom lines might involve helping students think and behave more like democratic citizens. *Ethical* bottom lines might emphasize valuing other perspectives, working for civil rights for all people, and protecting the planet. Some teachers' answers focus on issues of *social imagination*, such as creating community, becoming careful listening friends for others in the classroom and the world, and fostering loving kindness and compassion. *Academic* bottom lines promote authentic reading and writing, dynamic habits of mind, and students' sense of self-efficacy as learners. Finally, there are bottom lines that center on *disciplinary goals*—thinking and problem solving more like disciplinary experts (scientists, writers, social scientists, mathematicians, and so on).

For their units on voice, Jeff and Sarah identified similar goals:

1. Everyone must be noticed and included!
2. Everyone has to see themselves as a person of immense potential in terms of personal development and personhood, as well as having the capacity to learn about and contribute to conversations about voice.
3. Everyone has to develop the ability to serve others, help others tell their stories, and encourage others' voices.

Articulating their bottom lines helped Jeff and Sarah test out and consider the ways in which what they were doing each day was or was not serving those bottom lines. The existential questions themselves and the culminating projects required everyone to tell some of their unheard stories and to be listened to and noticed. Both students and teachers were required to notice, listen, and advocate as part of the unit's work.

Sarah and Jeff made a rule that they would notice each student personally at least once a week in a way that was unrelated to academics. The rule prompted them to notice students' new haircuts, ask students about their extracurricular activities, and just ask individual students how they were doing. When we notice students personally, we model for them how to notice others in ways that recognize the whole person. We demonstrate that we see them not simply as students who fill desks in a classroom, but as people who are all inherently learners in the process of becoming more mindful and whose learning is shaped by personal experiences, observations, and literacies that may not be privileged in academic settings.

Noticing students personally is a means of enacting bell hooks's (1994) concept of *engaged pedagogy* with its emphasis on teaching "in a manner that respects and cares for the souls of our students [which] is essential if we are to provide the necessary conditions where learning can most deeply and intimately begin" (p. 14). Noticing them sends our students the message that we value them as whole people, and therefore that we value their unique perspectives and contributions to the conversations that we take up in our classes. It is also a way of modeling for students the ways they can notice one another and listen each other into fuller existence (O'Reilly, 1998).

Jeff's and Sarah's units also foregrounded the pursuit of personal agency and honoring the agency of others (this relates to cultivating the dynamic mindset, which we explore in the next chapter). Both teachers thought hard about how to use language and feedback that promoted a sense of effort attribution and agency, in part by using procedural feedback: causal statements highlighting effort and the use of strategic tools. In procedural feedback, the responder first describes what the learner/author/reader has done strategically. Next the responder unpacks the effects of the strategy use, then feeds forward to describe what could be done next, perhaps providing tools for this effort. Improvement and growth is ascribed to effort and strategy. For example, Jeff responded to one student's story draft in this unit in this way:

> I read the first draft of your story. [Describing/Noticing what the writer did]: Your characters were fully-formed, each had a problem to solve, and were clearly influenced by the setting. So while generating your characters, you must have put the effort in to make good use of our WAGS (World of the character, Actions of the character, Goals of the character, Stakes to the character) protocol. [Unpacking the effect of the strategy]: The characters seemed to rise like holograms from the page for me and it was clear how the setting either invited them or disinvited them to use their voice! [Feedforward about what could be done next/what is not achieved *yet*]: But I am not sure I understand the stakes faced by the two major characters, and this keeps me from fully feeling their dilemmas about whether to tell their stories, so you could go back to the WAGS and think about what is at stake for both and how you can show that in the story without directly telling us.

And a response using procedural feedback for a draft argument from another student:

I read the first draft of your argument. [Describing/Noticing strategy use]:
Your claim was arguable, debatable, and significant, so you must have put
the effort in to run a plus-minus-interesting protocol on the claim. And you
have evidence that is clearly related to the claim, so we can see how the claim
was generated from data. [Unpacking effects]: This was useful in beginning
to convince me to consider your claim that people often silence themselves.
But I found myself resisting you somewhat. [Feedforward]: So I wonder if
the evidence is sufficient to convince a reluctant audience, and wonder if
using our semantic scale tool would help you to think about finding more
evidence to convince a reluctant audience.

Jeff and Sarah's use of procedural/causal feedback, combined with student storytelling of agentive narratives, arguments about voice, and follow-up reports and
process analyses describing how they did their work foregrounded the second bottom line (what absolutely has to be achieved with students): Everyone has to see
him- or herself as a person of immense potential—potential that is in their power
to actualize through effort and strategies.

Sarah and Jeff both noted how easy it was to get distracted and not to pursue
their bottom lines. They developed the mantra: "Don't let yourself off the hook!!!"
They admitted to themselves how easy it can be to lose sight of the bottom lines
and to just try to get through the day.

We often ask our students what their own bottom lines or wishes are for a
particular class, school year, or their education as a whole. Although many of their
answers are expected (prepare me for college or a job, help me earn money and
support a family), just as many are inspiring and illuminating. Some of the most
memorable answers include wanting to be a better person, getting along better
with others, making a contribution to the community, noticing and embracing
the wonder of the universe, or helping solve the world's problems. Student bottom
lines are often attached to specific issues, such as learning how to help those in
poverty, learning how to help immigrants, or learning how to work for food safety
or against environmental problems.

We like to create vision statements for our classrooms that include these kinds
of goals, based on in-class negotiation with students. We publish them on anchor
charts in the classroom as a daily reminder to us all of what we are working toward, and that we are, in Boise State Writing Project fellow and teacher Andrew
Porter's words, "going after big fish and moving *really big* rocks!"

Referring to these charts as we pursue our work offers an ongoing visible reminder of the third space that we are cultivating wherein teaching and learning
happens in service of students' immediate and overarching life goals, as well as
the goals and aspirations of the community as a whole. This changes the dynamic
of the classroom from playing "guess what the teacher already knows," where students feel they are doing the teacher's work, to one where the teacher is helping the
students—as agents—do their own chosen work. It also helps remind us and helps

us show students how what they are learning is in service, directly or tangentially, to what they have professed to value for themselves and others.

THINKING PARTNERSHIPS TO SUPPORT IMPLEMENTATION

We like to think of our classrooms as "thinking partnerships" where students, teachers, and community members work together to do things that we could not do alone, leveraging the unique social power of being together. We tell our students that everyone has to be a teacher who shares ways of doing what they are good at, and everyone has to find a teacher for challenges they are facing.

Pioneering research about teacher development (Tharp & Gallimore, 1990) found that teachers need exactly the same resources and supports that students need to transform themselves: vision and purpose, explicit assistance over time, collaboration, and a dynamic, can-do mindset. We therefore like to employ the same notion of purposeful, ongoing thinking partnerships with teachers. As we work with our inquiry and service learning initiatives, we try to provide multiple layers of assistance to teachers who are undertaking the work of reframing curriculum into inquiry, of integrating service learning into their teaching, and of meeting the CCSS and the demands of new assessments.

At the Boise State Writing Project, we provide institutes and workshops to assist teachers in meeting new challenges, such as those of the CCSS. We also provide ongoing thinking partnerships and mentorships where teachers who are experienced with inquiry and service learning (as just one example) regularly meet and consult with a few other teachers to assist them to combine an inquiry and service learning approach in their own teaching. Sometimes such work is given professional learning credit or even graduate credit.

Whether you have an organization like a National Writing Project site or a structure such as teaching teams or professional learning communities (PLCs) to support you, or whether you just team up with a partner on an ad hoc basis, you will certainly find it useful to articulate goals and to find like-minded fellow travelers and mentors to help you in your work over time. We often use the metaphor of a "running buddy." If you have a running buddy and regular rituals for training, you are much less likely to sleep in or skip a workout. Your commitment to someone else, or to several other people, commits you and assists you to complete the common project.

INQUIRY PLANNING PROCESS

Because Jeff has written full descriptions about planning and implementing inquiry units elsewhere (e.g., Smith, Appleman, & Wilhelm, 2014; Wilhelm, 2007; Wilhelm, Wilhelm, & Boas, 2008), we will only provide a brief overview here of the inquiry planning process for teachers with an emphasis on integrating service learning projects.

Framing Units with Existential Questions

Inquiry typically begins when a teacher considers her experience in regard to a curricular topic and then reframes that topic, typically with student input, as an existential question (Wilhelm & Novak, 2011)—that is, as a problem to be addressed and perhaps solved. Students are positioned in an agentive way, being invited to serve as novice disciplinary experts who have genuine contributions to make to the topic of inquiry. These questions push students beyond their usual ways of thinking or "playing school" by providing a framework to do what Angela calls "real work for the real world," as such questions naturally lead to service to self, peers, community, and environment. Pursuing such questions makes the material come alive in the context of students' lived experience, leading them to transformed ways of understanding and being that can work toward transformative cultural change.

Existential inquiry means helping students enter into thoughtful conversations with one another and with other perspectives in ways that deepen understanding and lead to various levels of service. Existential inquiry is being "alive" to and present with one another—listening to each other, actively eliciting and hearing other perspectives and stories and data, and cultivating our own evolving ideas into fuller existence. It is recognizing that knowledge is constructed by human beings and therefore mutable, and that generating knowledge is an ethical issue that requires us to be critical about its construction and effects.

Existential inquiry recognizes that teaching and learning are relational and occur in relationship—between teachers and students, between students, among all learners and experts in the field, and among learners, ideas, and their applications. It foregrounds teaching for understanding and use, social action, and service.

Identifying Unit-Level Goals

Though planning can proceed in different ways, because the elements of a unit are symbiotic and mutually supporting, we typically next identify one central conceptual and one central procedural goal for the unit. The conceptual goal is what we want students to *know* and be able to explain and justify by the end of the unit. The procedural goal is what we want students to be able to *do*, and is most often connected to a particular standard, such as writing a story with fully developed characters who are trying to solve a problem or composing an argument with a claim and supporting it with evidence and reasoning. We try to focus on only one conceptual and one procedural goal at a time because we want our units to be organic and coherently organized around a clear center. Related goals, or goals that need to be met in order to support these central goals, can be articulated later. In the initial planning stage, we want laser-like focus on what is most important, so we can be sure that these central goals will be met. These goals are focused on addressing the existential question, and are therefore necessary for identifying and completing culminating projects and service.

Additionally, we focus our goals because, as cognitive scientist David Perkins (1986) proclaimed, knowledge is a network. When we go after one central goal, all other related goals that are necessary, symbiotic, or in service of that central goal will also be reached, without checking off long lists of standards, which fragments curriculum. When Judith Langer (2001) of the Center on English Learning and Achievement (CELA) looked at literacy programs that excelled, especially with struggling or marginalized student populations, she found that such programs were highly coherent. Students understood the few big goals that were being addressed, valued them, and saw how daily learning activities were in service of these few valued goals.

In our work with teachers, we have found that units organized around one conceptual and one procedural goal actually end up meeting most if not all of the CCSS anchor standards, in ways that are highly coherent for both teachers and students.

Sarah's goals (see **Online Figure A**) provide a strong example of how central goals can be in service of answering an existential question and develop knowledge needed for a culminating project, as well as how one central conceptual goal and one central procedural goal immediately lead to meeting other goals.

Identifying Culminating Projects

Once we have articulated our unit-level goals, we identify a culminating project that is a form of canonical composition, such as an argument, informational text, or narrative, as defined in the Anchor Standards for Writing by the CCSS. We put this project in conversation with our goals. How will the project require that students master and apply, in actual accomplishment, the goals we have articulated? If the requirements cannot be met, then the project and goals are revised so that they align tightly.

We then brainstorm for service learning projects that will require and reward the goals of the unit and that will in some way address the problem posed by the existential question. These service learning projects should be both (1) ongoing throughout a unit (e.g., service to self and self-regulation by monitoring one's own learning and learning processes through formative assessments or peer responding by assisting others in composing and revising their writing) and (2) should result in some kind of culminating collaborative effort of the kind described in Chapter 1.

Even though we brainstorm our own ideas for service learning applications when we start planning a unit, we always involve students in identifying and developing service learning ideas as well. It's almost a truism that our best ideas and the best adaptations of ideas come directly from our students. Sometimes we withhold our own ideas until the students have put their oars in, but we like to have some ideas of our own to help guide our planning and to make sure that our existential questions can lead to service learning.

In Sarah's unit, the students brainstormed different kinds of service to pursue throughout and after the unit. For example, under the category of service to peers, i.e., providing direct services to classmates and schoolmates (which we explore in-depth in Chapter 4), students brainstormed ideas about how to express an open attitude, learn to actively solicit the stories and perspectives of others, share the stories of others, and help those who are unheard to tell their own stories. Students identified the need for practice in noticing those who were silent or marginalized, ways to question and prompt to elicit stories, ways of listening, and ways of telling stories.

This planning approach helped Sarah consider assignments and activities that would teach students how to listen to themselves (quieting the internal editor) and others, and how to elicit stories from others through uptake, follow-up and mirror questions, restatements and requests for elaboration, and the like (Wilhelm, 2007). Sarah's students composed problem/solution arguments around issues of identification and being heard. Then they moved to address issues of being heard and exercising voice by writing "calls to action" in the form of PSAs. Finally, students pursued service learning associated with these calls to action, most notably by composing problem-solving guides to help immigrants and refugees navigate the community and school cultures.

Frontloading and the Instructional Sequence

Once the goals and culminating projects are articulated, we can proceed with the backwards plan (Wiggins & McTighe, 2005). Specifically, we need to know where students need to be at the end of the unit so that we can plan instruction that will lead us from where our students are at the beginning of the unit (more novice) toward our goals (where students become more engaged and expert, masters of the central conceptual and procedural goals, and able to transfer and apply these in new situations). We also need to know how to give students the assistance and practice that they need over time to develop the new concepts and strategies necessary for completing the culminating projects, including service learning (expert application).

Such an instructional sequence begins with frontloading: prereading and prewriting activities that motivate and engage the students, that activate what they already care about and know, and then build upon this to prepare them for success on a task that they could not successfully complete without the assistance and practice that will be provided throughout the unit. Frontloading leads to a careful sequence of instructional activities, including readings, collaborative work, informal writing, and the like that will build knowledge step-by-step and provide practice in developing new strategic capacities that are necessary to the work at hand and in the culminating projects.

The importance of frontloading cannot be overexpressed, because the importance of motivation cannot possibly be overemphasized (Smith, Appleman, & Wilhelm, 2014; Wilhelm, Baker, & Dube, 2001). Motivation is the continuing impulse to engage and learn, and is prerequisite to the sustained work and practice required to pursue inquiry and to master substantive concepts and strategies such as those promoted by the CCSS.

Frontloading activates prior interests and knowledge. It also uncovers assumptions and misconceptions that students may have about a topic that are important to articulate because this foregrounding makes these misconceptions imminently more susceptible to correction and accommodation. As George Hillocks has personally expressed to us: All learning proceeds from the known to the new. If we do not activate students' prior interests and knowledge, then we have no resources for learning and there can be no traction for moving into new understandings.

In Jeff's unit on silenced voices (Existential question: Whose story does not get told? Why is this and what are the effects?), he provided frontloading by reading the local newspaper with his students, starting with the sports page. Whose story was being told? It looked like that of the local football team. Sure, there were some quick facts about the team's next opponent but this was not the story. Why? Because the audience of the Boise newspaper would be most invested in stories about their local team. The class looked up coverage in the local newspaper about the team's opponent and found a very different story and emphases. The class then turned to the front page and found a story about President Obama's foreign policy. By consulting foreign press coverage online, the students found much more positive coverage about the president and his policies. The class asked why this might be and brainstormed why the foreign press would have a more tolerant angle on the president.

The class continued going through the newspaper, even asking whose perspectives were shared in various comics, and whose were not. *The Family Circus* was mostly from a child's hopeful perspective. *Pearls Before Swine* provided a counternarrative, exposing the undersides of stories and personality traits (the Croc's greed, Rat's self-interest, Pig's obtuseness, Steven Pastis's self-mockery) that are typically hidden away as embarrassing.

They then turned to the American literature anthology in Jeff's classroom and looked at the colonial period. Whose story was being told? The American colonists. Whose story was not? Well, there was one Native American chant, which did not comment at all on the issues addressed in the colonial literature and documents, but seemed suspended in a decontextualized space. There was also no representation of the Tory perspective, nor that of the British or King George. In fact, all the writing was for the patriots and against the British loyalists. Jeff and his students discussed how such one-sidedness worked and what it worked for and against. Throughout the unit, students asked what and whose story was being told, which and whose stories were not, and hypothesized about why that might be.

Just as there is a dialectic between the existential question and the goals and projects, there continues to be a dialectic between the instructional sequence and the culminating projects. Teacher and students will revisit and revise the plan and critical standards for culminating projects, including service, as they get new ideas throughout the process of their learning.

Sarah's unit plan also proceeds from frontloading into a sequence of activities that builds students' conceptual knowledge about identity and voice, and procedural knowledge about how to argue step-by-step until students have the content and the strategies down for writing an argument. Sarah exhibits "pedagogical content knowledge" (Shulman, 1986) as she knows how to teach kids how to read for main ideas, how to construct texts for meaning and effect, and how to craft a powerful evidence-based and reasoned argument (see **Online Figure B**).

Toward the end of a unit, it is time to begin composing the culminating project and implementing a more substantive kind of service to the community that builds on the service to self and peers. Throughout the project, the students are engaged in an ongoing process of monitoring/reflecting—which is absolutely essential to consolidation and transfer—in which students articulate transferable principles of practice and set a future agenda/action plan for applying what is being learned in future contexts.

Finally, we advocate public sharing of the work, and making it archival in some way (sharing our work at a family and friends night, or making our work or presentations about the work available on the Internet, for example). We often conclude our work each quarter by having students present their work to one another. Once a year, we host a Night of Inquiry in which teachers share their inquiry and service learning projects with the wider community and our Boise State Writing Project community.

Whatever you decide to do, we recommend that you share your work with other professionals because doing so provides you with feedback, provides inspiration and models to others, and generally furthers the professional conversation. Besides, we think it is important to celebrate our educational experiments and to savor the work we have done and the learning that has been achieved. It is also a good reflection for us to name what worked and why, as well as the challenges that emerged and to consider how we might better meet those challenges in the future.

TEACHING WITH A SENSE OF URGENCY

Why are we so dedicated to teaching with inquiry and for service? The demands placed on our students are always growing. The problems we face in the world are becoming ever more complex. Such issues are both local and global: They affect both individuals and communities and the globe as a whole. The yardstick for success is no longer just local-level improvement because we live in a global world and economy. Information and knowledge are rapidly created and disseminated. What is most worth learning is learning how to learn, how to frame problems and pursue solutions, and how to apply what has been learned. This approach leads to flexible individual achievement as well as group achievement in a rapidly changing world.

Which of our students does not need to become more literate, to develop more problem-solving and coping skills, to become more community-minded? Who among them cannot benefit from collaborative, problem-oriented work and providing benefits to others? This is why we teach in the way that we do and why we do so with a sense of urgency. We are dedicated to helping our students navigate real-world challenges and rehearse to navigate real-world challenges in the future.

INQUIRY, WISDOM, AND SERVICE AS TRANSACTIONAL

Dewey and Bentley's *Knowing and the Known* (1949) made extraordinarily large claims about the importance of spreading transactional mentality in the modern world. As opposed to "self action," where "things are viewed as acting under their own powers" and "interaction," where "thing is balanced against thing in causal interconnection" (p. 108), "transaction" brings about "mutual understanding" and "turns differences to mutual advantage" (p. v). It affords us nothing less than "the right . . . to open our eyes to see . . . together." Without transaction, modern life "has been and still is chaos and nothing more" (pp. 68–69, 136; Wilhelm & Novak, 2011, p. 14). Existential inquiry is "transactive" in just this way and is addressed not just to the mind manipulating and re-creating the world but to the transpersonal elements of the human beings that are an integral part of the world and who are renewed by renewing the world.

It strikes us that all aspects of wisdom involve the interpenetration of "I" and "you" into the "us" and creating "third spaces" of possibility. And, of course, one of our most powerful tools for inquiring, for understanding one another, for building and deepening our conceptual and procedural understandings, and for becoming a community is the process of respectful dialogue: genuine conversation that involves listening and being heard. Dialogue is the essence of inquiry that leads to any kind of meaningful service, whether to self or others. We cannot be transformed without such transactions. Why would we not teach in such a way?

CHAPTER 3

Service to Self

The Dynamic Mindset

All instruction must involve service to self. After all, how can we call something "learning" if it does not lead to self-regulation and independence, to understanding new ways of doing things that can be applied right now and in the future, both in school and out? In this chapter, we will explore how every unit can and should include activities that lead to self-regulation, self-care, accountability to self, and personal problem solving; to knowledge transfer; and to the development of personal empowerment through the cultivation of a dynamic growth mindset.

SERVICE TO SELF AND WHERE IT LEADS

Every teacher has probably heard students ask: "Why do we have to learn this stuff?" This question is a cry for education to be personally meaningful and functional in immediate and compelling ways that are obvious to the student.

Jeff has many times been guilty of telling students: "You'll need to know this when you get to 12th grade/college/Mr. Strohm's class next year" or "You will thank me when you get to college/professional life/and so on." He's learned through hard experience that these kinds of arguments are not persuasive and that his students *won't* thank him—at that moment or later on.

Both in their research on the literate lives of young men (Smith & Wilhelm, 2002) and the lives of passionate readers of marginalized texts (Wilhelm & Smith, 2014), Jeff and Michael Smith found that students wanted an immediate functional value to their learning that was personal and that led to personal competence, action, and function in the world, whether externally or in terms of "inner work" and emotional/psychological growth, particularly in regard to becoming the kind of person that they were striving to become.

In a unit based on the inquiry "Is war ever necessary?" Jeff began during the frontloading phase by asking his students, "How do you think this unit might possibly be personally meaningful to you?" Toby, a 7th-grade boy carrying several labels, including learning disabled and emotionally disturbed, had this to say:

> To be a good citizen you have to think about when the government should go to war and stuff, and whether you should support it. But I think I am a

lot of times going to war with other kids and maybe this will help me think about when to stand up and when I should just chillax.

Toby's comment demonstrates how he made a meaningful personal connection to the inquiry question. We maintain that inquiry-based teaching allows teachers to explicitly encourage and assist students to always search for personal connections and implications of their learning.

At the end of the unit, Toby reflected on his learning:

> I used to think that war was never necessary and that fighting with other kids was never necessary—even though I did it. I guess I still believe that, because now I see there are lots of ways to think about it, and also many ways to "fight" that I had never thought of—like with Mandela or Martin Luther King—they were fighting and had good reasons to but they fought in lots of ways that I would never have thought of. It makes me want to learn more about ways of fighting that are not physical or violent that might lead somewhere for me and everybody else other than more fighting.

Toby's insightful comments show a student who sees real-world implications for what he has learned, and he is positioned to continue thinking about the application of his knowledge.

Through "service to self" activities, such as Toby's personal reflections, students' sense of accountability and independence as learners and civic participants grows, because they come to recognize that they are part of something larger and that they have the possibility and capacity to engage in ongoing cultural or disciplinary conversations and problem solving. Of course, this service work can be extended to thinking about the stories we tell about ourselves and others. How are these stories of possibilities? How do they work imaginatively toward growth? How can we reframe stories and reflect on them in ways that will help us grow from thinking about both our own and others' lived experience?

This, in turn, leads to a consideration of personally vital questions such as: What is my odyssey, my existential quest? How does it intersect with others'? How might I pursue my own human journey to better connect to and transact with others and the environment in transpersonal ways? Perhaps Toby's quest will involve finding ways to maintain personal boundaries and work for justice in healthy and mutually respectful ways.

To start, it's essential for students to see that their current inquiry is about something that affects them personally and compellingly in direct or perhaps more tangential ways. They need to recognize that the issue framed in the existential question is something socially significant and that they personally have "skin in the game." This means not only knowing that they are affected by this issue, but also knowing that they can participate in better understanding and addressing the issue. We can then work to make visible the ways in which students are part of an ongoing cultural conversation and how they have the agency to act in ways that revise or extend that conversation.

The inquiry itself involves an introduction to the cultural conversation and a mindset development that helps students see they can assume a substantial voice in the conversation. Then they need to do the learning that is necessary, both conceptually and procedurally, so that they develop something to say and contribute functionally as part of the conversation, and know how to say and do it. Assisting students in achieving these conceptual and procedural goals is the purpose of the instructional sequence.

THE ONGOING DISCIPLINARY OR CULTURAL CONVERSATION

In Jeff and Michael Smith's book *Fresh Takes on Teaching the Literary Elements* (Smith & Wilhelm, 2010), Jeff wrote about how literary themes must be understood as turns in an ongoing cultural conversation. This notion of entering a conversation applies not only to identifying and understanding key details and themes in literature and informational texts, but also to the notion of understanding the topic of conversations around an inquiry, and the various positions in relation to that inquiry topic and existential question.

We are not thinking of casual conversation here, but rather of a larger, highly significant, and ongoing disciplinary or cultural conversation—the kind of conversation that Kenneth Burke (1973) described in his famous parlor metaphor:

> Imagine you enter a parlor. You come late. When you arrive, others have long preceded you, and they are engaged in a heated discussion, a discussion too heated for them to pause and tell you exactly what it is about. In fact, the discussion had already begun long before any of them got there, so that no one present is qualified to retrace for you all the steps that had gone before. You listen for a while, until you decide that you have caught the tenor of the argument; then you put in your oar. Someone answers; you answer him; another comes to your defense; another aligns himself against you, to either the embarrassment or gratification of your opponent, depending upon the quality of your ally's assistance. However, the discussion is interminable. The hour grows late, you must depart. And you do depart, with the discussion still vigorously in progress. (pp. 110–111)

When students engage in inquiry-based learning, they must catch the drift of the ongoing conversation, and they must learn enough about the conceptual tenor of that conversation to have something to add. But they also need to learn the strategies and procedures of acquiring knowledge and how to engage in that conversation. The existential question introduces students to the topic of conversation and its importance. Frontloading helps them gain entry, and the instructional sequence helps them learn the *whats* and the *hows* of participating in the conversation. The culminating project is a turn in that conversation, or an action inspired by the conversation.

Throughout the process, students have opportunities to master services to the self, such as knowing how to effectively participate in an ongoing conversation, to express one's perspective in such a way that it can be heard. Frontloading and other strategies will contribute to students developing the necessary stances, capacities, and understandings (all services to self) for creating the culminating projects and service learning that are immediate contributions to the ongoing conversation as well as "archival turns"—by which we mean these are knowledge artifacts that can be stored electronically or otherwise be shared and used over time. But here's an important point: This contribution must be based on rich understandings that serve the self as well as meet disciplinary standards, and that are useful—to the self and others—when applied to the problem out in the world. In other words, the understandings developed in the unit must be applicable to life beyond the unit, and must be situated in the ongoing disciplinary or cultural conversation that tests and complicates the conversation.

One of the reasons we gravitate to Burke's parlor metaphor is because of how well it complements our argument about organizing curriculum around inquiry problems, and structuring units around existential questions. Recognizing how texts, data, and knowledge are parts of a conversation helps us avoid being too reductive and information-driven in how we express our evolving understandings, and also helps students interact with texts, data, and knowledge in agentive ways.

For teachers who embrace a role of helping students develop agentive identities, it is essential that we recognize the ongoing nature of disciplinary conversations and developments. Knowledge is not stagnant; it also reflects culture. As Jeff noted in *Fresh Takes*:

> Burke is not alone in recognizing how ongoing cultural conversations are generative. Polanyi (1979) demonstrated that the issues authors and narrators address are going to be culturally shared and culturally contested values and beliefs. These are the topics and themes that are available for debate and that are recognizable and accessible to readers. (Smith & Wilhelm, 2010, p. 156)

Because the issues are debatable, students develop a sense of agency. When Jeff's students explore the existential questions, "What are civil rights, and how can we best protect them?" or "To what degree is the American dream achievable to all?," they see how the question applies to them personally in the here and now. Because issues that come up are recognizable and accessible, students see their personal connection to the issues (How is this school violating my civil rights—and those of other students? How accessible is the American dream to me and my family—and to the refugee families in our community?), as well as the social and cultural significance of addressing them.

Gee (1999) made a related point about "discourse communities" and disciplines, which are kinds of microcultures. According to Gee, different themes/understandings are a focus of different cultures and subcultures:

> [If a text or data set] were not part of a larger conversation, as in Burke's parlor metaphor, it would not be compelling enough to write or to read: We write and read and think about topics of important debate at play in our cultural surroundings. Because themes/understandings are a part of an ongoing conversation, they don't provide the last word. Readers can choose to embrace them *in toto*; embrace them in part; or interrogate, adapt, or even resist them. (p. 116)

When students are moved in this way from learning information, from "playing guess what the teachers already know," they move toward participating as an agent and activist in ongoing conversations that require their input and service.

We want to encourage and enable students to participate in these microcultures; by inviting youth to be part of a conversation through service to self projects, we provide engaging opportunities for learning and knowledge creation instead of stale experiences in which students are required to memorize and regurgitate fixed sets of preexisting information.

CULTIVATING THE DYNAMIC MINDSET

Perhaps the most important service we can provide is helping students develop and cultivate a dynamic mindset. The dynamic mindset is a confirming attitude that one can learn, through effort and practice, to become more competent and proficient—enough to participate as a "novice expert" and eventually as an actual expert in the ongoing disciplinary conversations and the knowledge making and problem solving that is generated by these conversations.

At the Boise State Writing Project, and in our service learning initiative, we take this kind of mindset seriously, both for ourselves as teachers and for our students. We use the pioneering work of Carol Dweck (2006) and Peter Johnston (2004, 2012) to inform our work, and we urge readers to read Dweck's and Johnston's inspiring books in regard to the significance of such a mindset and ways to develop it.

Cognitive science supports the notion that all learners can learn what is next in their developmental journey if they are given a meaningful context of use (such as inquiry) and focused assistance and practice, over time, in that context. From Vygotsky's pioneering work (1962, 1978) to Benjamin Bloom's (1976) research on human potential to Dweck (2006) and Johnston (2004, 2012), the data make it poignantly clear: Learners learn if they have the attitude that they *can* learn, if they expend effort, if the learning is situated, and if assistance in mastering strategies is available. Our abilities are not fixed; they are dynamic. Anyone can master the next available challenge if they embrace their capacity to learn and if a few minimal conditions are met.

The dynamic mindset rests on the belief that intelligence and abilities are developed and cultivated with practice and over time. In contrast, the fixed mindset assumes that abilities and intelligence are static. The fixed mindset aligns with information-transmission models of teaching and the notion that students will either have the capacity to "get it" or not, because the curriculum is set in stone. The dynamic mindset aligns with models of sociocultural teaching with inquiry and for service, because the belief is that students can and will learn if they are assisted as they struggle through the learning challenges. In Figure 3.1, we provide a summary of the differences between the two mindsets.

We embrace the dynamic mindset and recognize how it helps us grow as teachers and helps us promote student achievement. The dynamic mindset undergirds all of our pedagogical decisions—and those of the teachers we feature in this chapter and throughout the book.

Developing the dynamic mindset is a direct way to provide service to self because it is a positive and empowered way to be in the world. It leads to persistence, dedication, practice, and mastery, but it's useful in other ways as well. For example, any kind of significant project, such as a service learning project, inevitably involves challenges. If we are incorporating service, we are always incorporating difficulty. We value Mariolina Salvatori's (2000) notion of difficulty as generative. We and our students turn toward difficulty instead of away from it; difficulty is an integral part of the learning process, and it helps develop the dynamic mindset and the future possibilities that come with this habit of mind.

Erika Boas's Food Unit

We now turn to a 7th-grade inquiry about food that Boise State Writing Project fellow Erika Boas designed and taught. Her instructional sequence exemplifies how a teacher can intentionally design a unit to address the required curriculum while also being attentive to students' real-life needs and issues—the perfect combination for service to self. Erika's bottom lines across all her teaching are to (1) develop a dynamic mindset in her students because "this will be doing them a lifelong favor—helping them to work towards their fullest potential and to believe in themselves, especially through inevitable challenges," and (2) develop a dynamic reader and writer mindset by "developing a metacognitive awareness of a strategic toolbox for reading and writing—procedures they can transfer and develop and use across a lifetime of reading and writing." In the case of her food unit, Erika was interested in developing what Wilhelm, Smith, and Fredricksen (2013) called a "strategic toolbox" specific to the reading and writing of informational text structures such as listing, summarizing, describing, process describing, comparing, cause/effect, and problem/solution.

Figure 3.1. The Fixed Mindset Versus the Dynamic Mindset

Fixed Mindset	Dynamic (or Growth) Mindset
Intelligence and abilities are static.	Intelligence and abilities are developed and cultivated with practice and over time.
Tends to lead to avoiding challenges.	Tends to lead to embracing challenges as opportunities for growth.
Tends to be defensive or gives up easily when faced with challenges.	Tends to be persistent in the face of setbacks.
Tends to see effort as something to avoid, as fruitless, or, worse, as demonstrating incompetence.	Tends to see effort as the path to mastery.
Tends to ignore useful feedback, regarding it particularly as negative—sees it as judgment.	Tends to learn from criticism, framing it in causal or procedural terms, using informing principles of how to do things more effectively in the future.
Tends to feel threatened by the success of others.	Tends to find lessons and inspiration in the success of others.
Learning goal tends to be to look as smart as you can.	Learning goal tends to be to learn as much as you can.
The most important information is whether one is successful. It shows who is smart and more valuable. "How" is irrelevant.	The most important information is "how" someone did (or could do) something, because that's what we can learn from.
When encountering difficulty, view the difficulty as failure, question one's ability, assign blame for failure, and cease acting strategically.	When encountering difficulty, engage in self-monitoring and self-instruction, increase strategic efforts, and don't see self as failing. Instead: "I don't have it quite *yet.*" Consciously build a toolbox for problem-solving success. See learning as a process in which shortfalls are necessary parts of the process to achieve success and deep understanding.
When asked, "When do you feel smart?" say things like "When I don't make any mistakes," "When I finish something fast and it's perfect," or "When something is easy for me, but other people can't do it."	When asked, "When do you feel smart?" say things like "When it's really hard, and I try really hard, and I can do something I couldn't do before" or "When I work on something a long time and I start to figure it out."
Everything is about the outcome.	Allows people to value what they're doing in the process of doing it, regardless of the outcome.
When teaching, asks questions such as "Can I teach them?" and "Can they learn?"	When teaching, asks questions such as "How can I teach them?" "How will they learn best?" and "How can I assess to show progress and attribute it to effort, specific strategies, and practice?

Adapted from Dweck, 2006, and Johnston, 2012.

Erika chose to pursue this unit because food and nutrition fit the 7th-grade curriculum. She was also concerned about her students' eating habits in and out of school, their lack of awareness about the consequences of these habits, and the related body image issues among her students. The unit coincided with a paradigm shift in the school toward healthy eating, which won the school an award for healthy cafeteria choices.

She framed the unit with the question, "Are we what we eat?" She thought this question would grab her students by the throat, so to speak! But she also translated it as: How does what I eat affect me, my family, my local community, and the environment? And why should I care? These compelling questions led directly to service: both service to self and, eventually, to others and the environment (see **Online Figure C**).

Erika designed her frontloading to provide her students' entrée into the ongoing conversations about healthy personal diets and the effects of food production—an increasingly intense and complicated cultural conversation. Erika began with a "See, Think, Wonder" activity (Wilhelm, Wilhelm, & Boas, 2008), providing students with several photos of families seated in their cooking area at home with a week's worth of food. The photos came from the book *What the World Eats* (D'Aluisio & Menzel, 2008). They included the Mustapha family in Chad, the Mastuda family in Okinawa, and the Revis family in North Carolina. Erika gave her students these prompts:

1. What do you *see* in these images?
2. What are you *thinking* as you look at these images?
3. What *wonderings* do you have about these images?

These three questions mirrored the trajectory of inquiry because the students had to identify salient data (what they saw), interpret and infer connections across the photos (what they were thinking), and be critical and applicative (their wonderings). This process is the very trajectory of inquiry: Notice the data, see patterns in the data, consider what the data mean and how this can be confirmed and applied.

Erika's students worked enthusiastically on the activity. As she noted:

I'm getting a two-fer here because not only are they seeing how different people around the world cook and eat—so we are building conceptual background knowledge—but they are also practicing moving from the literal (what do you see?) to the inferential (what are you thinking, i.e., what connections and comparisons are you seeing, what inferences are you making?) to the critical/applicative that leads to both further inquiry and to applications of service (what wonderings do you have?).

This is a strategic movement that reflects the process of knowledge making, and the path to wisdom that Erika takes up again in teaching her students questioning schemes in the context of the unit.

After completing the See, Think, Wonder activity, students shared their work and circled the most compelling words and phrases in order to create choral montages (Wilhelm, 2012a, 2012c), a powerful technique for identifying key details and for beginning to interpret these as students share their thoughts and wonderings and begin to articulate their thoughts about the most compelling ideas that are coming up in their reading and inquiry.

Keeping track of their food intake and asking questions about it not only stimulated an attentive stance in students, but also helped them practice skills that will benefit them in future research-based writing contexts as they move toward mastery of the next generation standards. The food log did not ask for a simple report of what students ate but rather demanded reflection, inquiry, and a move to begin situating knowledge within a larger cultural conversation. The processed foods activity encouraged the same kind of thinking, positioning students as agents in their learning process while guiding them toward increasingly nuanced inquiry. (See **Online Figure D** for food log and processed foods activities.)

Pursuing Conceptual Goals and Service

After the frontloading, Erika dove into the unit with a substantive reading of an excerpt from Pulitzer Prize winner Michael Moss (2013), "Exploiting the Biology of the Child," from *Salt, Sugar, Fat*. She used a "Directed Thinking and Reading" activity (Wilhelm, Baker, & Dube, 2001) to model, through a think-aloud, how to notice embedded informational text structures and key details in the piece, and how to use a three-level questioning structure to get after literal, inferential, and critical/applicative meanings (Wilhelm, 2007).

After Erika modeled the noticing and questioning strategies, naming tip-offs and rules of notice, she began mentoring by asking her students to help her generate noticings and questions using the strategies she had shared. Then students began to work in pairs to use the strategies more independently, as Erika moved through the classroom offering specific kinds of procedural and causal feedback, like the following comment: "I see how you are noticing the tip-off words that help you to notice key details, and that there is comparing going on, and you ask an inferential question about the comparison using a 'between the lines' question that will help you make an inference."

With her central conceptual and procedural goals for the unit in mind, Erika reflected:

> I'm trying to promote that dynamic mindset and reinforce the strategies
> they are learning and how these are helping them to provide "service to
> themselves." They are learning how to ask questions to comprehend at the
> literal, inferential, and critical/applicative levels, and also they are learning to
> notice key details and structural cues that help them navigate text structures.
> Of course, I'm hoping to shock them into seeing how they are manipulated

by food marketing and the food itself. If they can see how this is done, then that is a big "service to self." And of course, I am working to help them become more aware, and take some ownership of their diet, eating habits, and family eating rituals. That is "service to self" that extends to others and can serve them for a lifetime!

Erika's reflections illustrate how the learning that takes place in partnership with service is not confined to just one assignment or classroom moment. Instead, it's learning that stays with students long after they have completed the assignment and have left the classroom. It is learning with implications that don't merely sound good in theory; they are actualized in the real world.

Erika wanted her students to apply a dynamic mindset to the feature articles that they wrote later in the unit. This writing project allowed them to meaningfully use this mindset because effective nonfiction writing is about engaging the reader, posing questions, and sharing the most shocking points and statistics to encourage others' thinking and to work for new understandings and for change. Their level of engagement in the "service to self" project contributed to the quality of voice in their writing. Erika explained, "I really noticed that when the students were personally invested, then their writing had more of a unique voice and quality to it—the staking their identity idea."

As the unit continued, students completed jigsaw readings in which five groups read different texts and became experts who went to other groups to teach them about the key details, inferences, critiques, and evaluations of the reading and how it related to the inquiry. This was followed by more independent work, and, with assistance, the students pursued short research into personal eating habits, and then more extended research into cultural issues of food production and consumption. Students then created informational cards about hot topics and traded them.

They also created commitment cards that committed them to a "service to self" and a food guide (Figure 3.2) and podcast that allowed them to share the outcomes of their service to self with other students, parents, and community members. The guides were also archived online and in the school library for future use.

At the end of the unit, Erika asked her students to complete a process analysis in which they described what they had learned, how they learned it, and how they had worked through challenges. She also asked them to identify their expertise according to the standards of expert readers, writers, and disciplinary experts about food and nutrition. Finally, Erika asked the students to consider how they could cultivate ways of transferring and using what they had learned in service to themselves and their families, and how they would monitor and continue to promote this service.

Ultimately, though the unit focused on service to self, Erika's students were moving beyond themselves to think about how what they had learned could be of service to others, the community, and the environment.

Figure 3.2. Food Guide Back Cover

Not only was the unit a big success, but it also led to other forms of service. Erika became the lead author (with Jeff and his daughter Fiona) of a book called *FOOD* (2014) based on her inquiry.

In addition, other teachers have been inspired to teach versions of the unit. Boise State Writing Project writing fellows in the service learning initiative subsequently proposed a one-credit course for teachers on food to critically consider the cultural conversation with fellow professionals.

So it goes: One great idea leads to another, but in this case, what is even more worth noting is how service can lead to more service—for both students and teachers working together on compelling and substantive issues. We have found this to be the case regardless of students' grade levels, as the following example from a 3rd-grade resource room illustrates.

Becoming Great Learners

In 2013 Sara had the opportunity to coteach a service learning pedagogy seminar to a small group of elementary-level preservice teachers. Sara, her colleague Faith Beyer Hansen, and the mentor teachers were there to support these undergraduates as they took their initial forays into teaching with service learning. All of her students were one semester away from student teaching, and were completing a 3-day-a-week internship at a nearby elementary school.

Rachel Kenneson, a dual special education and general education major, implemented a compelling service to self mini-unit with the 3rd-grade students in her resource room placement. Because many of these students with special needs struggled with self-regulation strategies, Rachel structured the mini-unit around the existential question "What helps me be a great learner?"

Rachel began the unit by reading her students Julia Cook's book *It's Hard to be a VERB!* The engaging book (to which her students could really relate) provided an entry point for a conversation with students about how it can be difficult to pay attention in school, especially for students with lots of physical energy. The outcome of their conversation was a student-generated anchor chart of ideas for what children can do to be great learners. As Figure 3.3 makes clear, the students were able to self-identify effective actions that they could take that reflected their growing abilities to self-regulate their behaviors. Some of the ideas they brainstormed reflected strategies the children had to learn to help control impulsive behaviors (e.g., playing with the squishy heart that the teacher made available) or to focus if their minds wanted to wander (e.g., by rubbing their heart with one hand and their stomach with the other).

By inviting the students to be part of the conversation about how to be a great learner instead of telling them what to do, Rachel guided her students to engage in service to self by being proactive. By engaging them in identifying, inventing and practicing strategies of attention, mindfulness, problem solving, reading, and writing, she helped them self-regulate as learners. The next step in Rachel's unit involved having the students specify two self-regulation strategies that would work for them.

The conversations that developed around the anchor chart led students to acknowledge how they often found it challenging to refocus their minds on learning after recess. Rachel recognized a teachable moment and introduced the students to three yoga postures and a deep-breathing exercise that helped them better prepare for learning. The children found the yoga postures and breathing exercise so effective that they wanted other students to learn these relaxing exercises as well.

Recognizing the opportunity to expand the unit from service to self to service to school community, Rachel set up a date for the 3rd-grade resource room students to teach her general education 2nd-grade students yoga as a form of relaxation. Seeing her students with special needs serve as leaders and teachers for

Figure 3.3. What Helps Me Be a Great Learner?

younger students was one of the highlights of her internship. Rachel's mini-unit demonstrates again how service can lead to more service and how students see how they are part of something larger by sharing their knowledge with an audience.

Reflection to Serve the Learning Mind

Reflective activities such as formative assessments, imaginative rehearsals for living and future application, learning to teach someone else, journals, and responses to guided prompts are an essential component of any inquiry or service learning approach. Robert G. Bringle and Julie A. Hatcher (2003) illuminated the interdependent relationship between service and reflection: "The definition of service learning also highlights the importance of reflection. Reflection is 'the intentional consideration of an experience in light of particular learning objectives'" (p. 84). Equally important, they noted, reflection activities create a bridge between service and educational content and allow students to study and interpret service just as they would read and study a text for deeper understanding.

Rachel's mini-unit on being a great learner is a stellar example of how reflection provides service to the learning self, which leads to service to other aspects of self as students acquire the habits of mind to be self-aware. Erika, too, embedded formative assessments into her inquiry unit on a daily basis, asking students to name what they had learned and what they still found challenging or confusing.

Whether they are connected to a larger service learning project or not, reflective activities of any kind are a means for students to make their reading, writing, and thinking processes visible for themselves. As they make their learning processes visible, they come to understand more about their needs and they can recognize places upon which they may need to draw and/or develop strategies for learning success.

For example, we find it effective for teachers at all levels to include a writer's note requirement throughout the process of composing projects (see **Online Figure E**). Throughout the process, students submit writers' notes wherein they articulate their goals for a piece of writing, assess their work in progress, name challenges, point to key choices they have made and why, and request feedback that will best help them assume ownership over their writing and achieve their desired goals. Notice how each of these steps asks students to inquire into their own composing in ways that align with CCSS writing standards. Students consider purposes, audience, planning, development, organization, and style in ways that are appropriate to task, purpose, and audience, and they consider the ways they are developing their writing while focusing on what needs to be strengthened. Depending on the type of text they are producing, they can also get practice using shared disciplinary terminology about writing.

The writer's note helps students gain a greater understanding of the composing process itself as well as their own writing that they can carry forward into future writing endeavors, an invaluable service to self. Any time we ask students to inquire into and reflect on their learning in meaningful ways, we are creating the conditions for service to self as students come to places of greater self-awareness and understanding of what their strengths and needs are as learners.

SERVICE TO SELF AS A GATEWAY

Any powerful inquiry unit necessarily involves service to the self in the ways Erika and Rachel so elegantly provide and promote. Transferable learning, such as that required by the procedural standards of the CCSS and the next generation of standards worldwide, requires that students learn strategies that they can use as readers, writers, and problem-solvers to pursue their own present and future learning—an independence that is a clear form of service to self. The conceptual knowledge that students develop should provide background knowledge for their future learning. But their learning should go beyond academic knowledge and the skills that they need in the school setting. Learning should open the gateway that enriches every student's sense of agency; their dynamic mindsets as people, readers, and writers; their sense of estimable personhood; to reflection and the capacity to know what one knows and how one knows it, and where one will go next; to more enlightened and wide-awake living. Erika's and Rachel's units do all of these things and more, and the service to self these units promote leads naturally to service to peers, classroom, school, community, and environment.

CHAPTER 4

Service to Peers

Fostering Supportive Learning Cultures

In Erika's food unit, she focused primarily on "service to self" in that she wanted students to learn transferable strategies of reading and writing. Of equal importance was their conceptual learning and its practical application as she wanted them to grow in awareness about what and how they ate, leading to more "wide-awake" personal choices and a healthier diet and lifestyle.

It's obvious that all real learning must involve some kind of service to the self, both in strategic and conceptual terms and in functional and metacognitive/reflective terms; learning is for understanding and use, for rehearsing, navigating, and solving problems through your own efforts—whether those problems have only personal dimensions, or community or disciplinary dimensions as well.

We would also argue that service to self involves developing the capacity to do "inner work," which can be understood as "the effort by which we gain an awareness of the deeper layers of consciousness within us and move to an integration of the total self" (Johnson, 1986, p. 13) in order to live a fuller, more wide-awake, healthy, and rich life for ourselves and beyond (Wilhelm & Smith, 2014).

We now turn to that "beyond." In this chapter, we focus on Angela Housley's friendship and community unit, which we briefly introduced in Chapter 1. Angela's unit was inspired by her desire to create community in her classroom and across her school for the benefit of all, but was rooted primarily in her desire to help students see how they could be of service to others. Angela had a special concern for students who struggle, or who were excluded or marginalized. Like Vivian Paley, she knew that marginalization was hurtful to everyone in the community, including the insiders.

In her unit "How can we be better friends and citizens?" her goal was for each child to contribute positively as the class addressed academic challenges together and solved classroom and playground problems of exclusion and marginalization. Angela's 4th-graders mastered literacy strategies and content while they developed personal strategies for relating positively to others in order to create community, for bracketing negative responses and emotions, and for cultivating positive emotions such as compassion in order to create an inclusive, supportive environment.

Although her work clearly cultivated service to self, her focus was on getting kids to provide—and to value providing—service to peers and to the culture of the classroom (and by extension, the school) by creating problem-solving strategies and protocols for inclusion and friendship.

A classroom episode involving Angela's student Willie, who has Asperger's syndrome, provides a poignant illustration of the lasting impact of this unit. Willie was chosen to be the presenter about a small group's inference as to why the wolf in a folktale would be the one to eat the witch. He had to state the inference as a claim, provide evidence, and then give the group's explanation of how the evidence fit their claim, thus practicing argument while making a complex implied relationship inference. Angela noted how the group members were

> trusting enough to let him speak for them—patient enough to let him do it with their help. Willie usually doesn't want to speak or present, but when he does they try and let him and act as his lifeline only if he asks. They don't let him do everything he wants, they treat him like anyone else, but they include him and let him do what was going to be hard but not too hard.

This kind of culture of community support does not happen by accident. It happens through the careful cultivation of service in the classroom, and the valuing of others and their perspectives and experiences. Says Angela, by way of coda, "I can get everything done academically for my kids that I must do and get service done, too, in ways that help get the academics done and a whole lot more. That's why I teach."

TEACHING AS CREATING CULTURES OF LEARNING

Throughout our work in the Boise State Writing Project service learning initiative, we discuss the importance of creating and sustaining particular kinds of learning cultures. Angela is especially devoted to the notion that teaching must move from a culture of reception to a culture of meaning production, something Jeff has argued long and hard over the past 15 years (Wilhelm, 2007; Wilhelm, Baker, & Dube, 2001; Wilhelm & Novak, 2011). Angela defines teaching as the creation of a culture of learning, cooperation, encouragement, and support. Such a culture, she believes, "assists the students to become better learners, better thinking partners for one another, better citizens."

Angela explained that this culture of apprenticeship and meaning production requires:

> developing attitudes such as the "dynamic mindset" as well as attitudes of experimentation, curiosity, exploration, and even something that I might call divergence or creative quirkiness . . . so you have to pay attention to how you talk about things and how you accept, value, and reward student thinking versus what Jeff calls "playing the game of guess what the teacher already knows."

The movement from information transmission to that of a sociocultural apprenticeship into expertise is exactly the focus of the CCSS and the next generation of standards and assessments internationally. But making this shift can be a challenge for teachers, and sometimes for students.

The culture of helpful apprenticeship that Angela creates makes collaboration a necessity—"because we are smarter together than we are alone, and because big inquiries and problems require everybody's participation." The collaborative stance puts students in touch with one another and classroom visitors, and combines ideas, processes, and projects that don't typically go together in order to serve "a common project and the common good."

The helpful apprenticeship approach embodies the idea that diversity brings vitality to a culture, and leverages the social fact that people are together in a classroom. Angela explains, "I want to do things in my classroom that require everyone, that the students could not do on their own." In this kind of culture, students are active participants in making choices, shaping, and transforming the learning environment, and taking on an ethos of responsibility for themselves and for the community, both in the present moment and into the future.

Angela believes that "cultures [of learning] are created by learners—including the teacher as a fellow learner—and are created *by*, *with* and *for* each other," so learning becomes self-organizing and self-generating. Teaching in a culture of apprenticeship is about teachers collaborating with students in creating meaning through modeling, demonstrating, guiding, and assisting, but always through creating the evolving structures and ethos of the classroom (Wilhelm, 2007; Wilhelm, Baker, & Dube, 2001; Wilhelm & Novak, 2011).

Learning involves mastering strategic processes that involve practicing (as novice experts), applying, reflecting, refining, practicing more, and applying some more, always moving toward more expertise as readers, writers, problem-solvers, and also toward becoming compassionate thinking partners and citizens. Learning in this regard always moves students toward closer correspondence with actual expert activity.

INQUIRY AS INDUCTING STUDENTS INTO COMMUNITIES OF PRACTICE

One of the many attractions of inquiry is that it inducts students into a problem-solving community akin to what cognitive scientists call a "discourse community" or "community of practice." Students first take on the mantle of the "novice expert," engaging in what Lave and Wenger (1991) called "legitimate peripheral participation," working toward the community's goals and taking on ever more responsibility and independence as they gain more conceptual and procedural expertise through the collaborative work of the group and the practical guidance provided by the teacher (a nearby expert) and more distant experts whom they may watch in videos or read about in books.

Learning happens, in this view, when people engage in the significant meaning-making practices of the communities in which they participate, including clubs, sports, religious and social organizations, and family or friends. Lave and Wenger (1991) indicated how in school we think of learning in terms of disciplinary communities. That is, in science classes, we consider how to think and problem-solve in the ways of the scientific community; in art and music classes, we envision the community of artists; in mathematics courses, we focus on mathematicians, and so on. This necessarily involves social interaction, e.g., learners are involved in group-work, use peer assistance, negotiate and share what is learned, participate peripherally but legitimately in larger communities of practice, and become inducted into the values and practices of those larger communities or disciplines.

Communities of Practice

When students engage in a classroom project as "novice experts," they try out new kinds of actions, master new concepts and processes in an authentic context, and try out new "possible selves" through different ways of behaving and being. This behaving and being pertains to the academic, but, as Angela is quick to point out, is also intrapersonal and interpersonal.

As novice experts, students are trying out new community identities, seeing what it is like to be an editor or a scientist or a person in authority, as well as a helpful friend or relational problem-solver. They can learn about and take on to some degree what can be called the "epistemic frame"—the perspective and way of knowing from the expert's community of practice—developing and taking on the knowledge, the perspectives, the affiliations, and commitments of that community.

As Jeff (2010) wrote in regard to developing wisdom:

> It strikes me that all aspects of wisdom involve the interpenetration of "I" and "you" into the "us" of a new and new kind of community wisdom, that is, involves creating "third spaces" of possibility. And of course, one of our most powerful tools for inquiring, for understanding each other, building and deepening conceptual and procedural understandings, and becoming a community, is the process of respectful dialogic conversation. . . . (p. 55)

The conversations students have are not just with teacher and one another, but also with texts and with distant disciplinary experts as they engage ideas through discussion, research, and writing.

Angela's Bottom Lines

Angela was articulate and passionate about her bottom lines. Her primary bottom line is that her students should become mindful community members, recognizing that every community member has strengths and weaknesses and that everyone has an obligation to the whole community. She teaches her students that, as mindful community members, they have an obligation to include everyone and to help all their peers be their "best possible selves." Along with that, her students learn that everyone is interdependent and therefore must look for ways in which others can help them as well as actively look for ways to help others. Everyone has a voice, and for Angela, creating spaces where those voices can speak and be heard is critical. She frames writing in her class as an important place where students can exercise their voices and share what is important to them.

Angela's notions of community, collaboration, and interdependence permeate everything she does throughout the school year, not just in the unit we feature here.

As one example, she begins each day of the school year with "morning meeting." This, she said, "keeps getting better every year, and every day of each school year—it's magic." The idea of a morning meeting comes from the "Responsive Classroom" philosophy (see www.responsiveclassroom.org)—but Angela and her students have really made it their own, and they continue to remake it each year. Each day starts with the meeting, which begins with greetings, followed by a group activity, sharing, and the morning message. Angela notes that morning meeting:

> is a place to practice the conceptual and procedural knowledge
> that we are developing as well as practicing ways of being together.
> We are always bringing forward questioning techniques, how to
> notice key details, or whatever we are learning—so the activity is
> practice in all these things: We are always practicing the language
> part of how words and sentences work to communicate, to foster
> the dynamic mindset—it also sets the tone of the day.

Angela prioritizes morning meeting because of its academic benefits and its role in helping students collaboratively build a classroom community. The morning meeting is an essential feature of the purposeful instruction that Angela designs to achieve her bottom lines. Even in the midst of a "bubble year," when she had a class of more than 30 4th-graders in a room that provides a better learning atmosphere for 25 of fewer students, Angela prioritized morning meeting. "Especially with this number of kids, we have to build community," she asserted.

Existential Question

For this past year's unit, Angela's question was: How can we be better friends and citizens/community members? She was quick to point out how the question changes with each group of students, emerging organically from their expressed concerns about interacting—a subject that always arises. Angela's subquestions usually address ideas such as, "What is a good friend? How do you make friends? How do you stand up for others? How can you turn enemies into friends? How can you be a friend to someone who needs a friend? How can we become unlikely pairs and groups to foster diversity?" But, as she pointed out, those are the questions that tend to naturally emerge for her students; they are not questions that she predetermines.

Frontloading

Angela is spontaneous about frontloading. Children consistently bring issues of friendship and citizenship to the classroom. As Angela said:

> Inquiry and service learning is about addressing problems that already exist! You don't need to make up problems or tests—the world is filled with them. The kids' world is filled with them—so they are already engaged—and you can teach everything you want to teach in that context.

For example, students might discuss how a football game was unfair or how someone won't work with them. Angela uses her students' experiences as the catalyst and the frontloading. She then organizes and foregrounds things by noting what she hears and has been hearing, and she and her students make an anchor chart of the problems, exploring why the problems exist and how they can work to understand and do something about those problems.

Angela identifies her job as integrating what she must teach in terms of curriculum and standards with her students' concerns. If, for example, students complain about conflicts on the playground, she has opened the inquiry:

> Hmm, it seems like we have a question here about how we can all have fun on the playground. This is about how people treat one another. What is recess for? What is the classroom for? What is fair? How do we treat everybody fairly, especially if soccer and football take too much space in our postage-stamp playground?

The next step would be to measure the playground, think about the space that different games require, consider who wants to play what kinds of games, and examine the mathematical ratios to devise plans for fairness.

Students are then engaged in interdisciplinary work, doing math, problem solving, and learning civics all at the same time. Angela notes how they regularly deal with such issues, but there comes a time during each school year when she pauses to have students list their concerns and work together as a caring learning community ready to inquire deeply into these issues. Students' voices matter to Angela, and she treats them with respect that reflects her stance that they are co-creators of knowledge and community.

In a pioneering study on the socialization messages provided to elementary children (Brint, Contreras, & Matthews, 2001), the findings revealed that 84% of the socialization messages to students were about "basic organizational controls" related to keeping order in the classroom and getting academic work done. (In fact, in two-fifths of the classrooms studied, these were the *only* codable socialization messages!) Only 11% of the messages were about "regulation of self and the self's relation to others" (p. 161). A mere 1% of messages were about fairness/justice, responsibility, and self-control. Courage and honesty scored at .9% and .6% of messages, respectively, and values such as individual uniqueness, respect for group differences, and respect for own group culture received hardly any notice at all.

Angela was not okay with these findings: "Most of the messages in a classroom have to be about substantive issues like how to be, and how to be together. Doing an inquiry unit on friendship and citizenship focuses our attention on these matters." Her approach ensures that teacher-student and student-student messages are about these issues rather than the organizational controls that Brint and colleagues (2001) identified as the prevalent socialization messages in elementary classroom dialogue.

Online Figure F features a template for Angela's inquiry unit, with an emphasis that this is not an exhaustive example; rather, it highlights only the major pedagogical moves that guide the inquiry and help students as they perform service to peers.

Instructional Sequence

As in all cases throughout this book, we highlight here only a few of the basic instructional moves made by the teacher.

Angela begins the unit with a whole-class reading of the district mandated health book. The class reads about family, intellectual, emotional, and community health, making notes about what is necessary to health and how the students can help one another achieve good health. Along with the health book, the class reads informational texts as students "jigsaw" and share with others their separate readings of a series of books about character traits such as responsibility, honesty, and loyalty.

As students read and share what they are learning, Angela shows videos that explore friendship. One of her favorites is a CBS news video from an elephant sanctuary where a particular elephant is befriended by a dog. Angela asks the students to describe their relationship and when the students maintain that they are friends, she points out that they are making a claim.

She then asks, "How do we know the elephant and dog are friends? What is your evidence?" The students say things like "Because they care about each other," to which Angela prompts, "How do you know that?" When students respond, "Because they helped each other," Angela further pushes student thinking by asking for an example. Angela records the students' answers and asks, "So what you are saying is that if people do these things like help each other, then they are friends?" This constitutes evidentiary reasoning, as required by the CCSS and by expert practice in any field.

Angela also shares pictures and photographs and asks her students to provide other images that illustrate friendship. Students learn to pay attention to details and which details about relationships are important to notice, and then they connect those details back to friendship. By guiding students to identify details about relationships and putting them together in summaries to identify main ideas, Angela is using the topic comment strategy (Smith & Wilhelm, 2010) that requires students to identify the general subject of a text and the comment made about that topic by the arrangement of details. These thinking and discussion skills are transferable to reading and writing for the main idea.

With every activity in her class, Angela always asks what students think (claim), how they know (evidence), and so what: An explanation of how the evidence supports the claim (reasoning). She believes in her students intellectually: "The kids are capable of this, and when they do it, they are making inferences, sometimes at a really complex level." The students then work in small groups on creating Frayer charts, graphic organizers to help define central concepts. They continue to work on their Frayer charts in small groups and as a large group throughout the unit. Angela engages students in a variety of reading, writing, and problem-solving activities throughout the unit, but here are a few of her favorites.

Angela likes using activities such as "Significant Lists" and "List-Group-Label" to build knowledge (from Wilhelm, Smith, & Fredricksen, 2013). She provides a list of items that could be associated with friendship such as a movie ticket, birthday invitation, pizza, and candy. Then she asks what they might all have in common with friendship (e.g., they are all ways of sharing together and usually involve an overt invitation to share). She then asks students about items that don't fit on the list, such as "spelling test," and asks students how this could be made to fit (e.g., ask someone to study with you for the spelling test).

Students bring in physical objects and artifacts that they associate with friendship, tell their stories, and look for commonalities. The class then groups the items in various ways, with the goal of continuing to define friendship and identify what Angela calls "friendship moves." With a more refined definition of friendship mapped out, students then compose friendship oaths for other students using what they have learned from the Frayer charts and about "friendship moves" (Wilhelm, Smith, & Fredricksen, 2013).

To help students more effectively problem-solve, Angela engages students in an activity called "Four Corners/Spirited Debates" and "Value Lines/Vote with Your Feet" (Wilhelm, 2012a). She begins with the personal identity question, "Are you a morning person versus night person?" Students then walk to a pre-identified corner of the room that best fits their identity. Angela wants them to recognize differences in personal preferences, thoughts, and behaviors so students can learn to identify, respect, and negotiate differences. She asks students, "Can different people be friends? What would you have to do if you are a morning person and go to bed early and one of your friends is a night person?" Students discuss solutions and write journal entries in response.

When Angela uses "Vote with Your Feet," she provides a solution to a friendship dilemma. Students vote by taking a place on a continuum of how willing they would be to try that particular solution. She also pushes students to propose their own solutions. She'll ask questions such as "Should your friends always eat with you at lunch? Never to Always." After they've voted with their feet, Angela asks, "What makes you say so? So what?" Students practice basic argumentation related to friendship—developing the kinds of academic skills that are outlined in the CCSS in the context of an inquiry that matters to them.

Activities like these help students identify observations about friendship to add to their Frayer charts about how to act like a friend—laughing, playing outside, having fun, and sharing together are examples. Angela asks them what they have to do to make this happen in the classroom and beyond: "If friends have fun together, share together, then we have to invite one another to do things." This includes being willing to "help one another with challenges, trust one another, be willing to share, and then we talk about and rehearse strategies for doing these things."

Students create and act out drama scenarios about relational problems; write friendship picture books based on these scenarios; read and write narratives; create informational texts such as lists, comparisons, and definitions; and write simple arguments about friendship and citizenship—activities that develop lifelong strategies and that meet the goals of the CCSS.

Angela explains, "[D]oing one activity helps them do the next—and everything is related to the inquiry about friendship and about service to peers—how we can be better friends to others, even those we don't know or who are different."

Reading a Shared Central Text: Cynthia Lord's *Rules*. As students move to reading a shared central text, Angela continues to focus and assist them to

> paying attention to situations and details in our reading—what is it that
> we need to notice and how do we notice and unpack or infer about these
> details and how they are connected to other details—especially examples of
> friendship and nonexamples—but also for community and citizenship.

She reminds the students that communities can be small, such as a pair, a table group, or a team. *Rules* shows how a girl with an autistic brother becomes friends with an intelligent mute boy, using illustrated cards to communicate. In addition to enriching students' notions of friendship and community and practicing procedural goals, Angela uses the book as the way to introduce the students to one of their culminating service learning projects: the creation and use of trading cards about friendship, citizenship, and the "moves to make" to become better friends and citizens/community members.

If there is time, students form literature circles to read free-choice books such as *Friends Forever: A Secret Diary* by Margaret Clark, *Bad Girls* by Jacqueline

Wilson, *Being Bindy* by Alyssa Brugman, *A Year in Girl Hell* by Meridith Costain (a possible text for lower-ability readers), *Don't Call Me Ishmael* by Michael Baurer (also good for lower-ability readers), *Diary of a Wimpy Kid* by Jeff Kinney, or others. Students keep a journal about what they are noticing about friendship, what undermines or promotes it, and the like.

Culminating Projects and Service Learning. Her students are always excited when Angela says they will create trading cards. She begins by having her students share trading cards they have collected, and they begin to create a semantic feature analysis of what makes a good trading card. Angela supplements the class examples with movie trading cards, cooking trading cards, and football and baseball cards, and she also throws in some foreign ones. If the kids have not brought in Harry Potter or Pokemon cards, she shares some examples from her own sons' collections.

Students use this opportunity to study the cards and create a semantic feature analysis (SFA) of the cards: What are trading cards for? What do all trading cards do? What features do they share? How might they promote friendship and community? This activity familiarizes students with trading cards as a genre, and their SFAs become the criteria and critical standards for their own set of friendship cards, as pictured in Figure 4.1.

Students next write a definition of friendship, and practice writing microarguments about what good friends would do in problematic scenarios. Now they are ready to compose their own trading cards. The cards provide specific advice, language, and moves about solving relational problems such as how to accept invitations, how to decline, how to include someone who has been excluded, or how to notice if people are troubled. Students develop the criteria for the cards; honoring their individual voices in the requirements supports their commitment to the project and fosters the dynamic mindset.

The unit culminates with a trading card party. Each student makes 30 of his or her own cards to trade. Students evaluate their own cards in the context of their learning and the audience they care about most: their class and their peers. They experience the benefits of having an authentic audience; the party provides an opportunity for Angela's students to apply the skills they have been learning. Angela pushes students to reflect and rehearse: "You may not want someone's card—how do you respectfully decline? How do you gracefully handle being declined?"

In addition, the cards are archival; the class organizes them into chapters and puts an example of each card in two books, which are placed in the main office and with the school's counselor. When children from any grade come to the office or counselor with problems, they are invited to look through the trading card album to see if there is a card that offers a strategy or describes their situation. This reflective opportunity provides students with a chance to prepare for genuine dialogue with the counselor or office staff.

Figure 4.1. Friendship Card Examples

Culminating Projects as Service. Angela has students peer edit one another's compositions and trading cards using a "real friend" peer revision guide (see **Online Figure G**). Her students

> do really well with this because they have had so much practice with the substance of friendship and citizenship that they know what content should be there, and so much practice with the genre of a definition or argument or trading card that they know what features it has to have. And they know lots of techniques for generating content and shaping it since we've been doing it for weeks, so they know what advice to give one another.

Through their extensive experience in their community of practice, students increase their expertise and ability to participate intellectually and mindfully in disciplinary and real-world work.

At the end, students evaluate their own work with a 3-2-1: "three things I did well, two things I would change or add or extend if I had more time or a future opportunity to do this work again, and one aspect I am most proud of." In this way, students plan, practice, draft, finalize, evaluate, and transfer learning throughout the unit (Wilhelm, Smith, & Fredricksen, 2013). As a result, the students' compositions are "typically quite inspired and very good—this [peer response process] is another form of service to peers that we make possible through all the work we do together on reading, writing, and problem solving."

It's typical for the thrust of the unit to be played out for the rest of the year. In one class, the children clamored to create a playground user's guide with ideas for playing community-building games at home. The creation of such artifacts extended beyond the unit itself. The 4th-graders decided to develop cooperative games that maximized use of the limited playground space at their school. They put their math skills to work measuring the space and gathering authentic data to help them create guidelines for their games. The children consulted other user's guides to become familiar with the format and flow of these informational texts, helping them develop important literacy skills outlined in the CCSS.

In creating directions for their games, the 4th-graders went through the writing process to refine their product. The process included testing their games with 1st-graders, during which the 4th-graders were rewarded with positive feedback such as, "That was awesome! I want to play again!" They also had authentic "a-ha" moments when 1st-graders got confused or couldn't follow the directions; the 4th-graders got real-world feedback from the future users of their guide. The students joyfully approached the revision process because they knew that their work mattered. The end product was a delightful resource that the class shared with every family at the elementary school.

With such a strong emphasis on developing community and friendship and citizenship skills, Angela guides her students to serve one another through the conscientious creation of a shared space in which everyone thrives.

STRATEGIES FOR PROMOTING SERVICE TO PEERS

There are many other ways to promote service to peers that require less extensive preparation and instructional time. For example, in Jeff's middle school or college-level classrooms, he has long organized individuals and groups to be of help to one another. Students typically sit in home groups of four and serve as "homework partners" and provide support to help one another with homework, collect materials for an absent student, and generally look out for one another.

Jeff also asks students to sign up for both revolving roles and semi-permanent roles as "helpers" or "keepers." Revolving roles include being a classroom host/greeter who welcomes everyone by name into the class, class reporters keeping track of everything that happens during a day and publishing a summary, a sergeant-at-arms to keep time and make sure homework updates are available online, and a healthy snack provider. Semi-permanent roles include being mentors for new students, homework mentors, or workers in the school writing center or math center.

Teacher Emily Morgan does many of these things, and also has students keep "buddy journals" that are joint projects with classroom peers as they read and respond to one another's reading responses and writing, work on culminating projects, and the like. In addition, she has students keep buddy journals with elementary students and with student teachers and others who participate in their classroom life.

Emily has students write thank-you notes and cards to others during the year, always starting "close to home" to thank janitors, kitchen staff, secretaries, assistants, parent volunteers, and others in the school, and then the local community. She explained, "I want them to start thinking about their environment and all the people who help them and to think how they might be of help to them [the other community members]."

Emily asks students to engage in "random acts of kindness" such as moving outside their typical friendship circles to be of service to someone else at least once a week and to report it in their journals. She has students fill out "caught being nice" forms about teachers and other students to celebrate the acts of kindnesses they observe. All of these activities support Emily's classroom goals in and of themselves, but they also lead into an inquiry unit on understanding and valuing the perspectives of others.

Emily's unit on perspective is framed with the questions, "To what extent do we really understand the experience of people who differ from us in fundamental ways?" and "How can we work to achieve this kind of understanding?"

Throughout the unit, Emily has a different seating chart each day. When students enter the classroom, they get a "seat ticket." The ticket tells the student where to sit and has some conversational prompts or interview questions to ask the new person with whom they will be seated. There is also a deliverable to record in their journal that requires the input of that day's partner and often is followed by some sharing with the whole class. All of the questions have to do with perspective, and range from the casual (Would you prefer a mountain hideaway or a beach house? Why?) to the potentially deep (What would you do if you inherited a million dollars? Why? Or, What is your most significant soapbox topic—the most pressing world problem that excites you and that you want to address? Why?).

In one unit assignment, Emily asks students to pay conscious attention to something in their environment to which they usually do not pay attention, and to someone else who is present in one of their immediate situations to whom they usually do not attend. She asks them to journal from the point of view of that contextual element or person and to tell the story of various events and interactions from that perspective. Students document their mindfulness and what they learn from seeing from another perspective, and they reflect on the strategies they learn for attending to and appreciating other perspectives.

For example, one of these strategies is the "believing game" (Elbow, 1998) where someone believes the best of another person and her intentions. Another strategy is the "Annoying Game/Enriching Game" to identify how other people's behaviors or events/situations affect them by giving them some kind of negative or positive emotional charge. Students then journal about what it is in a situation or another person's behavior/actions that makes them feel that way. Through their reflections, they recognize why a particular behavior affects them, and also why that person might be behaving in that way and how the affected student might be supportive and/or differently responsive in the situation.

Emily also uses "hotseating" (Wilhelm, 2012a) to get students to imagine that they are a literary character and to respond as that character to various situations and questions. Students "reframe" and ask "What if it were otherwise . . ." to explore conditions in which they could be more understanding of others.

All the work that Emily's students do is in service of the procedural and conceptual understandings that are necessary to her class's inquiry into perspective (see materials from the unit in Smith & Wilhelm, 2010). The strategies they learn and practice can be used in a variety of situations or units to help students develop the capacities to be more understanding and supportive of peers.

ACTIVIST LEARNING THROUGH LOVE

There is a sense, in the work of teachers like Angela and Emily, that another given is the notion of the classroom as a space of caring and love. Service learning means learning through love and caring, not the touchy-feely kind but an activist love in service of promoting the concrete good in the lives of others.

In this chapter, we have provided portraits of service projects that seamlessly intersect such loving care with enhancing students' disciplinary learning and engagement. The collaborative classroom cultures that Angela and Emily foster for their students not only encourage caring communities through service to peers, but also provide service to the disciplines as students participate in inquiry, problem solving, and service in meaningful and creative ways.

Key to the creation of the collaborative culture of good citizenship that we see in Angela's and Emily's classrooms is the adoption of similar open, invitational stances that position students as already caring and already capable learners and community members who can become even more wide-awake helpmates to others. There is also the recognition that students are current as well as future participants in the creation of culture—the culture of disciplinary learning and of caring, democratic spaces in the classroom and beyond.

CHAPTER 5

Service to School

Creating Connections,
Creating Democratic Cultures

As the three of us discussed our own experiences as high school students, Whitney admitted that she never experienced much school pride. From her cynical teenage perspective, "school" was a group of students arbitrarily placed together because of geographical boundaries that someone had arbitrarily determined. Even though she served on the yearbook staff and wrote about various school groups and events, Whitney thought of school pride as a forced attempt to bring together a group of students who only attended the school because of where they lived.

Whereas Sara and Jeff felt more connected to their high schools, mostly due to their extensive extracurricular involvements, Whitney's view of high school is common among adolescents. Her memories serve as an important reminder of the need to provide opportunities that help youth connect to their school. After all, they spend roughly 40 hours each week there! Jeff often jibes that kids are in school for two reasons: Their friends are there, and it's required by law. Schools need to be places that students find not only safe, but also engaging, significant, and fun places where they want to be and where they engage in personally and socially significant work with other people that they could not do on their own.

Despite the antipathy that many students may feel about their forced attendance, schools are rich potential sites for community, for collaboration and research, for deep learning that can be pursued enthusiastically with something akin to joy. Jeff challenges the preservice and inservice teachers involved in BSWP programs to make sure that the unique social potential of the classroom and school is leveraged each day. He advises teachers, "Make sure that you are engaging students in activities that require us all to be together, and that require our complementary perspectives and contributions, otherwise the unique power and potential of school as a social space/third space is not being actualized."

As a site for service, school can function as a microcosm of the larger community and society, allowing students to develop habits of mind and engage in literacy practices that they can transfer to their participation as democratic citizens. At school, students can explore, map, participate, and practice enacting their knowledge and skills in an intimate context with which they are familiar and where they spend a good portion of their time.

To this end, many BSWP teachers have involved their students in community and school history projects.

DOCUMENTING SCHOOL HISTORY

Students can become actual historians when they are assigned school history projects. They conduct meaningful primary research, learn how the current moment has been shaped over time and by a variety of people and factors, build understanding between past and current students and teachers, and learn the value of documenting institutional memory. School history projects create a third space wherein students serve their school communities and develop research, analysis, and writing skills that are central to the next generation of standards and assessments like those associated with the CCSS.

School history projects serve the larger community, too, as Whitney's memories of a lost school history illustrate. She fondly remembers her elementary school in Roy, Utah: two buildings separated by a large asphalt playground. The front building housed 1st and 2nd grades, the school cafeteria, and the gymnasium, and the back building contained kindergarten and 3rd- through 6th-grade classrooms. Built in the early 1900s, the front building served as the original site for the elementary school. Old wood doors with paned glass windows and brass doorknobs with keyholes, brass coat hooks in the hallway, and the smell of a building with history—Whitney remembers the intimate details of the building where some of her most important educational experiences took place.

Although most of her later elementary school years would be spent in classrooms in the newer back building, she always loved going to lunch or physical education in what she and her peers called "the old building." In 6th grade, she and a friend discovered a hidden door behind the curtains on the gymnasium stage, and opened it to find a room filled with shelves of roller skates—the kind that used metal keys to adjust the fit. Their curiosity led them to continue exploring the building that they thought they had known so well, and they discovered a door that opened to a long, narrow stairway and into a basement filled with storage from the school's past. In those hidden spaces of the school, Whitney wondered who had been at the school before her, and when the old building became too small to accommodate all students.

During her college undergraduate years, the old building was torn down and a new addition was built onto the newer building in the back, leaving only a small parking lot in front. Although Whitney was in college, she was sad to see the beautiful historic building demolished, no longer a familiar landmark that she passed regularly. Even though Whitney did not experience what she would call school "pride," she was intensely interested in the history of her school as part of the community and her own place in that process.

Returning to Utah to visit family, she now drives past Roy Elementary and still feels a twinge of sadness. When Whitney thinks about the space that housed her and countless other students, she recognizes it as a rich research site with institutional memories worthy of preservation. Although she didn't have the opportunity to document school history in her own youth, Whitney intentionally provides opportunities for her students to document the histories of their schools. Many of our Writing Project fellows, such as Andrew Porter (Wilhelm & Novak, 2011), have followed the model in Figure 5.1 to pursue school history or ethnography projects, providing service to school by creating and sharing archival research documents and displays.

One of Whitney's students, Austin, compiled an extensive body of research as part of a school history project designed to document the history of the Women's Studies program at Marshall University. Austin's reflective excerpt illuminated what we believe is possible for students of any grade level to experience:

> It is my hope that this information serves as a useful starting point for anyone else interested in the history of WS [Women's Studies] at Marshall and with that goal in mind, I have structured this portfolio for ease of use. It will be made clear what information has been verified and what information has not. Any unknown information that I believe may present further research opportunities or require further verification will be indicated by red font and will also be accompanied by a short explanatory note if necessary to ensure clarity. Further discussion of potentially rewarding areas of research will be included in the reflection. If this portfolio serves as useful aid, to whatever degree, for any future research I will consider it a great success.

Austin saw himself as a participant in a larger and ongoing conversation. He valued his research not in terms of individual ownership, but as part of a continual shared process. He saw his project not as a finished project, but as a knowledge artifact that was extensible, revisable, transferable, usable, and archivable (see Wilhelm, 2007 and 2012b, for more on knowledge artifacts). In this way, knowledge artifacts are part of an ongoing dynamic, interpersonal process leading into the future. Austin did not define success based on his individual effort or project grade, but by how he shared and built knowledge with others and created connections among past, present, and future students. He saw himself as entering a conversation as a member of a "community of practice" in a "third space" of possibility.

Through guided reflection, students can situate their experiences in disciplinary conversations and consider how to apply their knowledge in broader contexts. Students then recognize how disciplinary conversations have application in and bearing on the world beyond school. School then functions as a place where focused knowledge making and transferable learning happen, rather than a contained place for learning information. They move beyond deterministic views of information to an understanding that knowledge creation is dynamic and ongoing.

Figure 5.1. School History Project Template

A school history research project guides students to research and document institutional history for purposes of preservation and/or analysis and as a springboard for future action. Research focuses on gathering facts about the school, creating a repository of written artifacts, and finding people from whom students can potentially gather oral histories. Such a project also requires students to "jigsaw" the research, to teach each other and help each other reflect and see connections across the different sets of findings, and then combine all of these findings into a coherent whole, representing and publishing this whole in some kind of archival electronic and multimodal document.

Essential Question: What is the history of our school, and how does this history reflect and/or shape the culture of our community?

Subquestion: How could the history of our school be used to transform the future of our school and community?

Guiding Questions

- What year did the school open, and what else was happening locally at that time? Nationally? Globally?
- How was the school name chosen?
- Who was the first principal?
- Who else has served as principal?
- Who were the first teachers?
- Who else has taught at the school?
- Who served as staff when the school opened?
- Which current teacher has taught at the school the longest and what changes have taken place during his/her years teaching for the school?
- What major policies have been implemented? For what purposes? With what effects?
- What events has the school sponsored? With what outcomes?
- What fundraisers has the school held? For what purposes and effects?
- What programs have been performed at the school?
- What significant athletic, artistic, or social and civic events are related to the school?
- What have teachers and students of this school gone on to do and what contributions have they made to the school culture, the local community, and the wider culture?
- What stories can school alumni tell us?

Prompts for Reflection

Through reflection, students consider their research, position themselves within the history of the school, see how they are part of something larger, and reflect on their ability to make contributions and/or changes based on the knowledge they have acquired.

- What contributions have you made/do you make to our school? This includes extracurricular activities (teams, clubs, organizations) as well as attitudes and behaviors in classes and hallways.
- What was most surprising in your research?
- What new questions has your research raised for you? What additional research could help you find answers to those questions?
- What connections can you make between your experiences and observations as a student at our school and your research?
- What did you think about our school before you started your research? What do you think about our school now?
- How has your school reflected and shaped community culture? Reflected or resisted larger cultural forces? Worked toward change and transformation?
- What resources are there in the school's traditions and history that could be used to move mindfully into the future?
- What was most valuable to you about the research you did?
- What might the research our class has done show about future directions for our school?

Sharing and Archiving Research

Projects may assume a number of forms, depending on grade-level abilities and the aims and scope of the assignment given. Typically the final artifacts involve electronic and multimodal elements. Some possibilities include:

- Collection of oral histories
- Repository of written artifacts (each artifact might be framed by student writing)
- Repository of other knowledge artifacts: videos, artwork, photo collections, music, and so on
- Permanent museum displays—both physical and digital—that make room for future students to add to them
- Performance piece for presentation to the school and/or community

Connections to CCSS and Next Generation Standards

Depending on the project, students might:

- produce clear and coherent writing in which the development, organization, and style are appropriate to the task, purpose, and audience;
- develop and strengthen writing as needed by planning, revising, editing, rewriting, or trying a new approach;
- use technology, including the Internet, to produce and publish various forms of compositions and to interact and collaborate with others; and
- conduct short as well as more sustained research projects based on focused questions, demonstrating understanding of the subject under investigation.

TEACHERS AND STUDENTS
AS DEMOCRATIC CITIZENS

In *Reflections of a Citizen Teacher*, Todd DeStigter (2001) defined democracy as "a way of interacting with others by which all people have the desire, ability, and opportunity to participate in shaping their individual and collective lives" (p. 12). As he further explained, democracy is "a process of associated living in which individuals participate in deciding what their world should be like, in acting to pursue these aims, and in sharing equitably in the consequences of that action" (p. 12). DeStigter's definition demonstrates that democracy (like the creation of knowledge artifacts) is an ongoing dynamic interpersonal process. Democracy requires collaborative inquiry, research, dialogue, and connection, all leading toward transformative possibilities. If we conceive of school as a microcosm of the larger society, then school is a democratic space where teachers and students are democratic citizens imagining new ways to interact in the current moment and in the future.

In "A Curriculum Framework for Active Democratic Citizenship Education," Ahmet Do'anay (2012) examined the National Council for Social Studies' list of qualities of democratic citizens, which we draw on, adapt, and connect to the CCSS in Figure 5.2. Effective citizens, as these qualities illuminate, are mindful, lifelong learners who engage in inquiry as a key literacy practice for participating in ongoing democratic conversations.

Service to school can further solidify the sense of association among students and accountability to themselves, others, and ongoing cultural institutions as they expand their vision of school and collaborate to foster a safe and vibrant school culture.

TRANSFORMING SCHOOL CULTURE

Robert D. Ramsey (2008) suggested that "[t]he definition of a healthy school culture has to be as fluid, flexible, amorphous, and adaptable as . . . well, as a healthy school culture" (p. 19). Although flexible in definition, a healthy school culture has certain attributes, regardless of context. Ramsey identified attributes of such a culture: It works for everyone; is principle-driven and values principles over policies; values connections, collaboration, and open communication; is a learning culture; prioritizes respect and each person's dignity; is fear-free or fear-reduced; and as a place of joy, is driven by passion. A good tool for examining school culture, Ramsey's list of attributes can be used to help students and teachers illuminate where change to school culture is most needed, and to ask existential questions that address curricular issues and standards in ways that will lead to service to the school (see Figure 5.3).

Figure 5.2. Qualities of Effective Civic Participants

Effective Civic Participants	CCSS College and Career Readiness Anchor Standards
• Embrace their responsibility for the well-being of themselves, their families, and their communities • Collaborate well with others and are concerned for the greater good	*They come to understand other perspectives and cultures.* *They prepare for and participate effectively in a range of conversations and collaborations with diverse partners, building on others' ideas and expressing their own clearly and persuasively.* [Students are better positioned to recognize their communities as diverse groups of people with a range of perspectives and needs. They are able to work respectfully and effectively with people from diverse backgrounds to foster the well-being of their communities.]
• Are knowledgeable about the people, history, and traditions that have shaped their communities, their country, and the world	*They build strong content knowledge.* *They comprehend as well as critique.* Students do not just learn surface facts but are able to inquire, make connections, and interrogate the "whys" and "hows" behind history and traditions.
• Continually seek information from varied sources and perspectives as they consider issues and move toward addressing or solving issues • Analyze and evaluate information they read, watch, hear, and see	*They value evidence and evidentiary reasoning.* [Students actively and inclusively seek to understand the different ways participants in a cultural conversation are situated, and understand that addressing issues and solving problems takes time and careful consideration.]
• Ask meaningful questions of themselves and about their world	*They demonstrate independence.* [Students take ownership over their learning as self-directed and lifelong learners. They see learning as an ongoing process that happens in and out of school and as a service to both self and others.]
• Address issues in innovative ways and develop creative solutions to problems whenever possible	*They respond to the varying demands of audience, task, purpose, and discipline.* [As independent learners, students are able to consider what's at stake and for whom when addressing issues, and can develop creative solutions by considering their audience, task, purpose, and disciplinary knowledge.]

Figure 5.3. Healthy School Culture Attributes

Attributes of a Healthy School Culture	Essential/Existential Questions for Inquiry
Works for everyone	For whom does the school environment work best; for whom does it not work as well? What can be done to make our current school environment work better for everyone, and for particular subgroups that might be marginalized?
Is principle-driven and values core principles over policies and procedures	What are the most important principles that guide our actions? What *should* be the most important principles guiding all school activity and decisionmaking? What would it take for us to act on those principles on a daily basis? How do we "do business" at school and how does this accord with our values and principles?
Values connections, collaboration, and open communication	What connects us to one another, regardless of how different we may seem? How can we draw on our connections to work together and dialogue across difference? How can diversity bring vitality and strength to our school?
Is a learning culture	What is learning and what encourages it to happen? What does an ideal learning environment look like? What would we need to do to create an environment that would allow each learner in our class to thrive?
Prioritizes respect and each person's dignity	What is "personhood" and how does school culture recognize and promote "personhood"? In what ways does school culture work against valuing and recognizing "personhood"? What does it mean to have dignity? How do we create a school environment where everyone has dignity and feels respected?
Is fear-free or fear-reduced	What fears do we have at school? How can we use our knowledge of fears to create a safer and more inclusive environment?
Is a place of joy and passion	What passions make me, me? What promotes engagement and joy in living and learning? What can school do to promote joy and passion in learning? How can we learn in a way that builds from our passions toward new ones?

Through service projects focused on transforming school culture, such as Angela Housely's 4th-grade students' efforts to promote friendship and caring and to reform the playground, students identify issues and problems at school, determine methods of intervention for addressing issues and solving problems, implement plans of action to shape a healthy culture for both present and future students, and take measures to increase the potential of the learning environment.

Inquiry into School Culture

Students talk a lot about school. Some of their talk focuses on their learning, but just as much focuses on the social experience in the halls and cafeteria and at recess. Lots of their talk involves critiques of school structures and activities.

When students are activist learners in conversations about school culture, they can move from complaint to commitment. Every critique opens a door toward working for change. Every complaint means they are committed to change, and therefore the conditions for deep commitment and connection to projects that develop new ways of "doing school" and "being in school" already exist. When complaints are reframed as problems to be solved, then students stand back and assume a new perspective from which to observe and interrogate the place where they spend hours each week. They assume an agentive and activist identity vis-à-vis the foregrounded problems.

A service project aimed at serving school community and transforming school culture requires teachers to value bringing students into all stages of the project as collaborators—from identifying problems and defining the scope of the inquiry, to engaging in background research, documenting findings, proposing, implementing, and studying the effects of various changes, and evaluating the level of success and setting a future agenda for themselves or others to take up. Students are treated as novice experts who are being apprenticed into disciplinary expertise and "third space" conversations as well as the possibilities of democratic life—a clear focus of the next generation of standards.

In Figure 5.4, we provide key questions for guiding students to articulate and internalize an existential question based on a teacher's observations of students and school culture.

Depending on the age and/or maturity level of students, the teacher may already have inquiry and social action options for a culminating project. But student ideas should also be solicited early on in a unit. These ideas become goals that can leverage the power of backward planning, because teachers and students can now plan what needs to be learned and realized in service of achieving the culminating projects.

Questions about possible service applications might be incorporated into brainstorming and class discussions that allow students to collaboratively generate potential solutions, actions to take, and documentation to produce. Regardless of approach, inquiry into school culture projects intersects seamlessly with CCSS

Figure 5.4. Service to School Project Template

Service to School Steps	Questions to Frame Discussion
Set the stage for inquiry	What do we notice as an issue or problem?
	When have you seen or experienced the effects of the problem? How did it make you feel?
	What is the context of the problem?
	What are the ways to reframe the problem so it can be seen from another perspective?
Make the problem matter	Why is the problem so problematic and worthy of attention?
	Why might it be important for us to solve the problem—for ourselves and for others?
	What follows as the consequences and costs of the problem? For different individuals and groups?
	Who benefits and who loses from the current situation?
Brainstorm action and potential solutions	How might the problem potentially be addressed?
	What challenges will be faced in addressing it?
	Here are some ways I've thought of for us to address or solve the problem. What are some other ways you can think of to address or solve the problem?
	Are there others outside our class who could also help address or solve the problem? If so, how can they help us? How can we contact them and solicit their input and help?
Decide on a course of action and break down the task into steps	What will we do to address or solve the problem?
	What responsibilities do we each have to help make sure our plan works? Depending on the problem, this might include daily, weekly, or monthly steps.

Service to School Steps	Questions to Frame Discussion
Establish markers for progress	What will be our signs of progress and accomplishment? How will we know when we are making progress in the short and long term, and how should we keep track of our progress? How will we know when the problem is adequately addressed or solved?
Document the results	What is most important about our project for us to share with others? How can we share what we have learned through our project?
Some connections with the next generation of standards (e.g. CCSS)	Students can: • Elicit and value multiple perspectives; • Converse and collaborate with diverse partners; • Consider and develop different problem-solving strategies; • Collaborate on creating real-world projects to address the problem; • Engage in short and extended research projects; • Explore their experiences with the identified problem and their ideas for solutions through drawing or writing opinion/argument pieces; • Share their opinion/argument pieces and participate in collaborative conversation to brainstorm potential solutions to the problem; • Reflect on their experiences and observations through drawing and writing as the project unfolds and they notice the impact of their service; • Make connections between the project and texts they are reading, comparing their points of view with the point of view of an author or narrator; and/or • Apply their knowledge about informational texts as they document the results of their service through the creation of informational texts for others.

speaking and listening standards that prepare students to effectively participate in conversation and collaboration with diverse partners. The scope of a service to school culture project can also address CCSS writing standards if students are assigned to produce different types of texts or to conduct short or sustained research as part of the project, and can address reading standards as well if students read documents related to their inquiry.

Thinking back again to the way she conceptualized school as an arbitrary grouping of students based on geographic boundaries, Whitney recognizes how the arbitrary grouping is one of the components that makes the potential for transforming school culture so great. Diverse groups of students, with diverse needs and perspectives, can work together to effect change, just as diverse citizens must collaborate to ensure a healthy democratic society.

Reading Made Real. At the junior high where she teaches, BSWP fellow Yoli Gonzales noticed a disturbing amount of bullying taking place. Her 8th-grade reading class had just finished a civil rights unit wherein they had read *The Outsiders*; during the unit many students revealed that they had experienced bullying both in and out of school. Yoli challenged her students with a succinct yet powerful invitation: "Let's do something."

With Yoli as their faculty advisor, six students started the Paw Out Bullying Club (the school mascot is a bobcat) with the aim to stop bullying through raising awareness and education about what to do about bullying. The club's membership grew from 6 to 60; included in its ranks were some students who had once bullied others. Part of the students' service involved modeling positive behavior for other students, such as assuming a friendly, inclusive demeanor by saying hello in the hallways to everyone, or asking others to stop bullying behaviors when they were observed. The scope of the project increased to creating PSAs, tip sheets for addressing bullying, and a play about addressing the issue of bullying, written and performed by students. The group also went on to make several public presentations about their work to "paw out" bullying.

Paw Out Bullying is a stellar example of a service project that positions students as agentive learners. What students experienced through their reading was not theoretical or distant from them, but real and close to home. Students subsequently transformed their school culture through an application of what they had learned and saw a marked decrease in bullying. Paw Out Bullying also shows how activist learning need not be limited to the school day. Extracurricular activities that emerge from the curriculum and/or school-based issues can intentionally help improve school culture and climate, as well as continuing to develop academic skills (e.g., as students-made public presentations).

Who Cares? Sometimes opportunities for service learning projects present themselves spontaneously. Shari Griffin, a 4th-grade teacher and a Wyoming

Writing Project fellow, unexpectedly launched a service learning project with her students. Shari recalls how it began:

> I noticed my annoyance over a sticky note in the hall. It was there when I went to the office and later when I went somewhere else and again on my way back. Then I realized I hadn't bothered to pick it up. . . . Why? Who would?

Shari decided to share this experience with her students, thinking that a simple collective conversation might lead them all to be more likely to pick up trash and create a cleaner and nicer school environment.

A simple conversation was not enough to satiate Shari's inquisitive students. Her 4th-graders had already been empowered through Shari's learning- and learner-centered approach to teaching; student voice and social action were honored, allowing the young learners to experience part of Todd DeStigter's (2001) description of democracy as Shari fostered their "desire, ability, and opportunity to participate in shaping their individual and collective lives" (p. 12) in the classroom. The students were so intrigued by the issue that they wanted to learn more about who did or did not pick up trash in their hallways—and why.

Shari embraced her students' interests and was confident that the as yet unknown teachable moments that would ensue were sure to directly address learning goals or could be connected to these goals. She trusted that authentic data collection and analysis would lead to conversations about civic responsibility and would help meaningfully address upcoming mathematics standards.

With Shari as the guide, her class designed an experiment: They planted various types of trash, ranging from snack wrappers to wadded notebook paper to Kleenex to Band-Aids, in hallway areas. Students took turns pretending to be reading nearby and kept data on the number of people who walked by and the number of people who stopped to pick up the trash. On the second day of data collection, the students started to keep track of the general age of the people who passed by—adult, intermediate, primary—because on the first day they noticed that younger kids seemed to be more likely to pick up trash.

Just like in real experiments, the 4th-graders' research design unfolded in response to trends in the data. Students learned how sometimes data bring more questions than answers. In their efforts to graph their data, the 4th-graders struggled to place data points such as the case of a special education paraprofessional who was helping a boy use his walker. Keeping the boy safe was more important than picking up trash, but how could the students plot that fact when they were seeking to determine who was most likely to be a good school citizen and pick up trash?

Rich conversations unfolded about responsibility. The students were taken aback by the idea that if there was something they didn't want to/shouldn't pick up (e.g., dirty Kleenex or a gross Band-Aid), then who should? Why should a custodian be the only person responsible? They explored questions such as: Why do people litter? Who should pick up trash? Why don't they? What might encourage people to pick up trash? Is there anything or any time that you shouldn't pick up trash? Rich conversations about issues of citizenship ensued as students developed the skills outlined in the CCSS for mathematics and language arts.

Shari's journey with her 4th-grade students illustrates how existential questions can emerge naturally, without prior planning by the teacher. The end result was students who were better prepared to analyze social issues and who cared enough about what they were learning to launch a campaign to clean up their school.

The Mockingbird School Community Project. Sarah Veigel guides her 9th-grade students to advocate for positive change in both school and community. When her students study Harper Lee's Pulitzer Prize–winning novel *To Kill a Mockingbird*, they learn to be mindful peer responders to one another's thinking and writing, and they pursue service learning projects that include schoolmates who might suffer from exclusion (Wilhelm & Novak, 2011). Their service projects extend beyond the school grounds to invite community members into the school who might benefit from an increased sense of community.

In Harper Lee's hauntingly beautiful novel, mockingbirds are innocent and vulnerable, making it especially wrong to cause them harm. Sarah frames the service project by asking students to consider who the mockingbirds in their school and community are, and how they and/or others might assume the role of Atticus, a just man who acts with empathy in a town that is rife with racial tensions. Learning in Sarah's class is couched within an ethics of responsibility: When one acquires knowledge, one has an obligation to apply it. Sarah asks her students, "When you know something, are you now responsible to transform yourself, to line your behavior up with what you know? . . . [D]o you challenge yourself to change your behavior?" (Wilhelm & Novak, 2011, p. 4).

Service on a Smaller Scale. Even when a teacher isn't able to implement a larger inquiry unit that focuses on service to school, smaller projects can still be integrated to create connections among students and to positively shape the learning culture. For example, in one of Whitney's classes, students watched Eve Ensler's documentary *What I Want My Words to Do to You*, focused on a writing workshop that Ensler facilitated in a women's correctional facility. In the conclusion, famous actors read the women prisoners' writing aloud, and the camera panned out to show each prison writer's response to the public reading of her work.

Whitney asked her students to use the phrase "What I want my words to do to you" as a springboard for writing their own pieces about the work they wanted their words to do in the world. Names were removed from the pieces and they were distributed so that each student was given another student's piece to read aloud.

Afterward, students reflected on how they had tried to "feel" the other person's words and perspective as they read, noted the intimate connection they felt to the writer, even without knowing who he or she was.

Whitney further probed students to raise questions about the connections they noticed between the "What I want my words to do to you" pieces and how they might draw on those connections in situations that required talking across differences to create increased understanding and a stronger sense of community in school.

Ethical Arguments for/with Service to School

Service to school projects are excellent ways to develop the habits of mind that are needed for considering, participating in, and writing ethical arguments (Smith, Wilhelm, & Fredricksen, 2013). When service is integrated into the curriculum, students' written arguments can connect to texts that they read as well as integrate research gleaned from primary sources, observations they have made, and their lived experiences. Students see firsthand the effects of thoughtful research and the consideration of evidence as their arguments become the basis for collaborative action that leads to positive change in the school culture.

Wayne Campbell Peck, Linda Flower, and Lorraine Higgins (1995) defined and examined the concept of "community literacy," a concept useful for thinking about the intellectual work we ask of students in projects aimed at transforming school culture. Arguing that a crucial but difficult step in community building is creating "an intercultural dialogue that allows people to confront and solve problems across . . . boundaries" (p. 204), they defined community literacy as "a search for an alternative discourse" much like a third space (p. 205). The four primary aims of community literacy are to support:

- social change that involves the use of writing for purposes of action;
- genuine intercultural conversation that allows people to dialogue across differences and seek diverse perspectives to work toward mutual goals;
- a strategic approach to the conversation, helping people as they develop new strategies for decisionmaking;
- inquiry that acknowledges the difficulty of empathy and joint action while examining the conflicts, assumptions, and practices that each person brings to the Burkean parlor (the ongoing cultural conversation) they are entering.

Projects focused on transforming school culture embody the aforementioned aims, acknowledging the inherent complexity of jointly solving problems in sustainable ways.

In problem-solving projects, students can discuss, research, and write about school problems they have witnessed and experienced firsthand, considering a wide range of explanations, evidence, and options. They also can adopt a reflective stance to consider the why and what behind their own assumptions and values in order to understand the ways their positions affect what they see and inform the decisions they make. Students then can begin to question the broader and ethical implications for their positions in relation to others. In short, students engage in the dynamic process of democracy through problem-solving projects.

In "The Rival Hypothesis Stance and the Practice of Inquiry," Linda Flower (2000) provided a framework for designing meaningful service projects that hone the skills necessary for democratic citizenship and understanding multiple perspectives (a goal of the CCSS and other next generation standards). When students consider rival hypotheses, they participate in "rivaling," a process that values a certain "*attitude* toward inquiry . . . [and] addresses problems as genuinely open questions" (p. 30). A strategic approach to inquiry, rivaling "seeks out other voices, alternative interpretations, and their supporting evidence" while generating rival hypotheses that 'challenge and conditionalize favored claims'" (p. 30). With multiple alternatives on the table, a group can move toward a consensual conclusion that has the greatest positive outcomes and that avoids negative outcomes for as many people as possible.

As a literacy practice, rivaling is ultimately an ethics of argument. It emphasizes the humanity of all stakeholders in a conversation and embodies the "power of softness" as students draw on their own and others' voices as they learn to "live for people rather than just for things" (Wilhelm & Novak, 2011, pp. 40–41). Researching and writing about real, collectively identified problems that teacher and students "care *about* [are] dealt with within an attitude of solicitous caring *for* one another" (p. 44).

Rivaling embodies the Common Core standards for writing, which value arguments that support claims in an analysis of substantive topics or texts, using valid reasoning and relevant evidence. Such arguments also proactively respond to competing arguments, which are highlighted by the process of rivaling. Rivaling also incorporates primary and secondary research to find relevant information from multiple sources, and calls on students to use their research purposefully with consideration of their audiences. **Online Figure H** provides the rivaling framework that we have used with middle and high school students to guide them as they generate arguments in consideration of the greatest good.

When students are asked to generate arguments through the rivaling method, the research and writing process can shift from an abstract, assigned academic stance to a concrete, lived accountability stance. Students learn the value of doing research to assume informed positions, recognize and genuinely listen to alternate positions, and make ethical arguments to advocate for changes that can have positive human and environmental consequences in their neighborhoods, communities, and society. These habits of mind are central to effective democratic participation.

FOSTERING COMMUNAL LITERACY PRACTICES

In a world where global connections are rapidly increasing and knowledge is made and shared in public, online spaces, making a shift to writing and research practices that emphasize collaboration is invaluable, if not essential. When conducted in the service of school, research functions less as an isolated, individual, and grade-driven endeavor, and instead becomes a dynamic and communal literacy practice.

Student writers experience an authentic sense of audience when they create texts and knowledge artifacts that represent their work, that speak responsively to others and to rival hypotheses, as these can be shared with school officials, parents, peers, and the local community. Through sharing their work, students can also teach and incite peers in other classes and grades to consider ways in which they, too, can provide service to the school to create a healthy, vibrant environment. Such texts and artifacts are visible signs of accomplishment and "proof positive of learning."

Students are also empowered through school-based research as they become experts on the cultural conversation and recognize their activist potential to transform culture through thoughtful inquiry that leads to planning, research, reflection, and action. When we think of some of the most transformative moments in history, we recognize that they all began with inquiry: Someone questioned the status quo or an injustice, or considered how to meet a challenge or need. Service to school projects teach students to ask *good* questions that lead to in-depth, meaningful research, innovative ideas, and creative solutions, developing habits of mind and ways of acting that are essential to a healthy democracy.

CHAPTER 6

Service to Community

Building Relationships for Democratic Engagement

We are inspired by Margaret Mead, whose resounding words remind us to "[n]ever doubt that a small group of thoughtful committed citizens can change the world. Indeed it's the only thing that ever has" (Institute for Intercultural Studies, 1999–2009). Throughout this book, we have advocated forms of service that foster the dispositions necessary for students to be Mead's citizens—for themselves, their peers, and their schools. We now turn to examine how students can, as mindful, empathetic citizens, apply what they are learning and what they already know to conversations in their local communities.

We want our students to have experiences that help them see that they are an integral part of the community and the community conversation, and that they can draw on their disciplinary knowledge to participate in those conversations. For example, in Whitney's class on women's rhetoric, students participated in a service project with the Women's and Children's Alliance (WCA), a Boise organization that serves community members who have been physically or sexually assaulted. Some students attended outreach events and learned how to adjust their approach to best engage the community audience attending a particular event. Another group of students conducted research on healthy relationships, creating Pinterest boards to increase the WCA's social media presence. Other students carefully read and analyzed the WCA's website, which the organization was on the cusp of revising, to ensure that it avoided victim language and emphasized positivity and the moving forward toward healthy relationships.

Reflection is a necessary part of inquiry, since it names and consolidates learning and cultivates a spirit of transfer for moving that learning toward future possibilities. Chris, one of Whitney's students, reflected on the service project and what he had learned about his community in his final writing assignment for the course. Chris wrote about his love of writing, situating it in new ways as he documented the responsibility and new possibilities he saw for language and writing:

> The responsibility of those precious words means everything to me. Through my work with the WCA, I've realized that words sometimes aren't just the product that is forged; they are the hammer, the anvil, the fire. We

make the words, but when they are put in the right situations they have the unique ability to go on to make a world of their own. Browsing through the WCA web page, I have listened to stories and read articles and felt pain and sorrow and hope in all of them. I have never met these people, perhaps I never will, but I know their words. I know their intimate and one-of-a-kind words, and through that I know them. That gives me investment; that is what I need to help intensify. The ideas that these words will hook people and will draw them in, and the better job I do and the bigger part I play, the bigger the dent I can make, and a lot of times it isn't a wrecking ball that causes changes, it's a thousand tiny hammer dents that topple the old ways.

Chris's inspiring reflections demonstrate his recognition that disciplinary knowledge could bring about change, both now and in the future. He saw himself as part of and accountable to the conversation on eradicating violence from his community. Service to community became something other than an assignment; it became a way of being in the world.

BUILDING RELATIONSHIPS

Keith Morton (2010) examined the potential and possible pitfalls of three frameworks for service to community: charity, project, and social change.

Charity-Based Service Frameworks. Charity is associated with an obligation to help, a form of "spiritually based service . . . that bears witness to the worth of other persons" (pp. 127–128). Although it is certainly positive, a charity framework typically involves limited service, such as taking a child's name from a community Christmas tree and buying him or her a gift. Though such service matters, it doesn't typically address the root problem or its cause, which, in the case of a community Christmas tree, might be joblessness and/or poverty.

Project-Based Service Frameworks. Process-oriented in nature, a project framework assumes "that no solutions are ultimate, and that thoughtful, reasoned approaches leading to measurable action—doing something—is the appropriate response to community needs" (Morton, 2010, pp. 129–130). Projects usually involve sustained collaboration with a community organization or group to provide direct service. Leadership skills, expertise, organization, securing resources, and encouraging the voices and participation of those served are central.

Social Change Service Frameworks. A social change framework "particularize[s] the general," grounded in the belief that "caring has to work in the particular" (Morton, 2010, p. 130). In other words, a general problem such as poverty is addressed in the specifics of a local context where community members collaborate with an ethics of care, for example, by working with families in a homeless shelter over time to provide tutoring or play time for children, or providing tips for structuring homework time, promoting reading, or providing cooking lessons to prepare the families for future life in their own home.

This framework is connected to community organizing and values "need[ing] to learn how we need each other" (p. 130). A social change framework is ultimately about relationship building, as people bring "their values, their actions, and their world into closer alignment with each other" (p. 131). Relationship building is the heart of democracy, as people strive to be empathetic, listen and dialogue across difference, ethically solve problems, and act with the greatest good in mind. Service to community provides opportunities for children and adolescents to be initiated at a young age into the relational process of working to promote social change.

Service as Relationship Building. Regardless of the theoretical or pedagogical framework, we believe that the best service learning projects are, at the core, about relationship building, just as we believe that all teaching and learning are relational and occur in and through relationships (Wilhelm & Novak, 2011). The approaches to service in the previous chapters involve ways of being in the world that are necessary for healthy, relational living in a democratic society. Service to community projects embody the learning and dynamic mindsets that all approaches to service promote and allow students to apply what they have learned in smaller settings such as the classroom and school to their communities beyond school.

Although the above examples differ in the type of service provided and the demographic being served, each project embodies a way of thinking that is transferable to building and maintaining relationships with others. If relationship building is the essence of social change, then large *and* small projects that consciously cultivate joy, love, caring, and the creation of possibilities for the self and others are implicit steps toward transformations of people whose ways of thinking and acting in the world are done in consideration of the greater good. The individual person recognizes his or her responsibility to the collective society.

Service to community projects demonstrate to students how education occurs both in and beyond the space of school. Students share their disciplinary knowledge and/or make new knowledge with community members, foster connections and accountability to their communities, and learn and apply principles of democratic citizenship as they create third spaces of service.

TEACHING AN ADVOCACY STANCE

As teachers, we have observed how some students initially are unable to identify issues that they are passionate about. These students seem to lack the belief that they are citizens with the ability to evaluate and respond to issues in informed ways. We might say that they lack the dynamic mindset. Such students can come to realize through guided inquiry that they are, in fact, invested in conversations about issues and problems that need to be solved and that they do have the capacity to learn and grow in ways that will help them make positive contributions toward solving these problems.

Teachers can move students toward an advocacy stance by having them complete an interest inventory in order to document the conversations to which they are already connected or in which they are already interested. An interest inventory asks students to list the activities they participate in, groups, clubs, and community organizations to which they belong or want to know more about, and trends that interest or concern them. Students can then begin to brainstorm important issues connected to each group or subject and what skills they have to help address the issues that these groups and the communities in which the groups operate face—as well as the skills they are willing to work to develop.

Alice Walker's (1998) wisdom provided inspiration to students who may have narrow views of what it means to be engaged in their communities:

> It has become a common feeling, I believe, as we have watched our heroes falling over the years, that our own small stone of activism, which might not seem to measure up to the rugged boulders of heroism we have so admired, is a paltry offering toward the building of an edifice of hope. Many who believe this choose to withhold their offerings out of shame. This is the tragedy of the world. For we can do nothing substantial toward changing our course on the planet, a destructive one, without rousing ourselves, individual by individual, and bringing our small, imperfect stones to the pile. (p. XXIII)

We want our students to understand that advocacy is not solely a component of large-scale social movements, but can also occur on a regular basis in small, conscientious ways that matter. To facilitate this understanding, we prompt students to brainstorm the ways they can advocate on a regular basis.

When they share their interest inventories with one another, students can recognize how advocacy occurs in relation to multiple issues and in a variety of contexts. In addition, they can understand the power of advocacy as a collaborative, community act as they learn how each member of a group brings different types of expertise, qualities, and strengths to bear as advocates on important issues. Democracy, as Dewey (1916) proclaimed, is indeed complementary—it requires different people bringing different interests and strengths to bear on a common project.

Interest inventories can also serve as a first step in helping students find a topic to research and then write an advocacy argument about. When possible, students can complete service hours with a community organization that addresses their chosen advocacy issues. Their research projects could involve investigating an issue or problem that directly affects the community organization with which they work, creating an advocacy piece, sharing it with the community organization and publishing and archiving the piece in some way, perhaps online, for future use.

Whitney remembers how one of her students, Andrea, embodied a spirit of inquiry and engaged as an advocate in ways she had not been assigned. Andrea served with an organization that provided free breast and cervical cancer screenings for women who didn't have health insurance. During that time, she also happened to be working at a local Mexican restaurant. One night when business was slow, Andrea discussed the services the cancer screening organization provided, and learned that the Hispanic women with whom she worked had never heard about the free cancer screenings. Andrea realized that a population of women was being excluded from a beneficial community service. She drew on her knowledge from the Spanish classes she was taking and translated the organization's brochure into Spanish so it could be distributed to the Spanish-speaking women in her community.

Andrea's story is an example of how students can intervene in community conversations as advocates. Our work as teachers and with other teachers who implement service learning makes it clear that her story is not an anomaly. When students are passionate about an issue or problem facing their communities, and when their teachers encourage them to take ownership over their learning, students of all grade levels can successfully apply their disciplinary knowledge and often go beyond the requirements of a given project.

REDEFINING POWER THROUGH COMMUNITY

In previous chapters, we've featured service learning projects that position students in mindful ways that help themselves and others. We want our students to see how authentic, meaningful power is not something we have *over* others. Power has meaning when it is shared *with* others to ensure the greatest good. Service to community projects are ideal sites for students to see how people of various ages, backgrounds, and interests can collaborate to address community issues and needs, as well as to see how they are integral parts of their communities, regardless of their age, background, or interests. Through such projects, literacy is not individual, but communal. Each person contributes what he or she can, based on his or her knowledge, abilities, and resources. Democracy is not about everyone doing the same thing; it is about conversation and complementarity (Dewey, 1916).

Whitney remembers well a powerful experience she had as a student that changed the way she thought about teaching, literacy, and community. Her memory helps frame how we can create the most generative service learning experiences for students. For a project in a women's rhetoric class, she and a graduate school colleague, Eric, conducted research on the women's suffrage movement in Nebraska. Their research experience was so exhilarating that they rarely spent time in the archives alone, preferring to work together as they continued to discover materials. Excited about the artifacts they had discovered, from newsletters to scrapbooks to a letter from Susan B. Anthony to a Nebraska suffragist, they wrote a traditional academic paper to represent their findings.

Through their collaboration with Judy, the owner of a Lincoln, Nebraska, theater company, Whitney and Eric learned how their research could be both academic and community-based. Judy wanted to commission a local playwright to write a play about suffrage to celebrate Women's Equality Day, and contacted the University of Nebraska–Lincoln English department to determine whether they had any students doing research on suffrage. Her original plan for a play on the suffrage movement in general shifted when she learned from Whitney and Eric that there had been a vibrant suffrage movement in her home state. Turning over copies of archival materials, notes, and the paper they had written, Whitney and Eric provided Judy with their contact information in case she had questions or needed them to locate additional artifacts for her play.

Whitney and Eric thought that was the end of their participation. They were surprised when Judy invited them to collaborate throughout the process, as she did with everyone who participated, including interested community members, the playwright, actors, costume and set designers, and archivists from the local historical society. When the first draft of the play was complete, everyone was invited to Judy's house for a conference call with the playwright and a first reading. Each person provided feedback and insights from their own knowledge bases as what came to be called the DeVoted Women Project came to fruition.

Solidarity and mutuality were natural project components because Judy encouraged participants to bring their knowledge and individual contributions to the table and valued that knowledge and those contributions. She exemplified the relationships that both John Dewey (1916) and Ellen Cushman (1996) called for when traditional power structures are eroded and forging interdependency among people is the critical goal. Rather than taking ownership over the project and directing it from the top down, Judy ensured all participants felt equal ownership over the project as it came to fruition.

Whitney's transformative experience as a participant in the DeVoted Women Project permanently changed the way she approached teaching, her role as a colleague, and her own community participation. She began to question how she could better recognize and tap into the existing interest, knowledge, and expertise that her students brought to the classroom in order to create a more communal classroom space. Power emerged through collaboration with her students. Everyone was positioned as both teachers and learners to create a more mutual environment.

Rather than creating a linear hierarchy that ranks and values participants based on expertise, projects like Judy's DeVoted Women Project are circular in nature; the idea or issue is central, and collaborative, complementary relationships form around it. The shift in what power means and what it can do when it is shared, as illustrated in the above example, shows what third space makes possible and how third spaces can lead to more innovative processes and projects. There are multiple ways in which we can set the stage for students to have these transformative experiences as they serve their communities and develop into the kind of democratic citizens who are equipped to compassionately, collaboratively, and complementarily address future social issues.

MAPPING THE COMMUNITY

In our experience, students are eager and willing to participate in service, but they are often unaware of what organizations and service projects exist in their communities or they are unsure of how to negotiate access into those organizations or projects. Versions of the "mapping the community" inquiry project outlined in the following pages have been pursued by various teachers in our Boise State Writing Project initiatives, spearheaded first by high school teacher Debra Smith. The project allows students to perform service based on their individual interests while simultaneously having them collaborate to teach one another about the bigger picture that is their community, thus providing service to peers in the process.

The existential question that forms the foundation for this project is: How does a community work to ensure that its citizens have access to the inalienable rights of life, liberty, and the pursuit of happiness proclaimed in the Declaration of Independence? Prior to providing service in the community, students read literary and informational texts that focus on the American Dream. Through class discussions, activities, and critical contemplation, they come to recognize the complexity of that familiar sentiment and question which American citizens' voices are heard and valued in the larger society and which voices are marginalized and excluded. In addition to exploring questions about the American Dream and the values, assumptions, and experiences students bring to bear on it, they can be asked to analyze craft, structure, claims, and evidence in the texts they read and subsequently write, meeting CCSS reading and writing standards.

Entering the Community

With a more complicated sense of the American Dream and happiness, Debra's students are prepared to enter their communities as more ethical, mindful citizens who critically inquire into community conversations. Service projects can incorporate the habits of mind that they are learning in school in order to become increasingly attentive to gaps in those conversations and to consider places where they can intervene to create change. As educators, we believe students are most empowered when they take ownership over their learning and recognize the importance of their contributions both in and beyond the classroom. As Debra's service to community project continues, students are invited to consider the conversation in which they've engaged about the American Dream and happiness in the context of their own communities. As they share the stories of migrant workers, refugees, the disabled, and others and their conception of the American Dream and the challenges to achieving it, they teach one another about community issues.

Though not absolutely necessary, we have found it powerful for students to conduct research to find organizations or groups in their community that address an issue or issues of concern to them, a short research project that is in line with the Common Core Anchor Standards for Writing. After their initial research, they can bring their findings to class to share as they decide where they want to pursue service hours.

Once students have decided on the organizations in which they're interested, we have often found it helpful for teachers to train students about how to make initial contact to get a sense of the feasibility of students' participation as volunteers and to begin building relationships with community partners for future students' service learning projects. Teachers can have students practice oral and written communication skills by having the students list key points to make when calling a community partner and writing practice emails that initiate contact. We couch these activities in Common Core writing, and speaking/listening standards that emphasize writing for specific audiences and purposes, and communicating and collaborating with different groups.

We have found that community partnerships are most effective when the community partner fully understands the learning outcomes, how the service is being connected to class assignments to enhance student learning, and what students at a particular grade/age level are capable of doing, and when students understand and help work toward the partner's goals. A partnership agreement like the one in Figure 6.1 provides written documentation for students, teachers, and community partners. Alternately, teacher and students can work together to compose the agreement document and action plan, giving students an additional opportunity to hone their rhetorical thinking and writing skills.

Students then work with their chosen organizations for a short or extended period. In the case of service to community projects, the actual service activities that students provide for an organization are less important than the fact that students become aware of a community organization and have the experience of working closely with it, and considering possible future services that could be developed and implemented in this context. Students can become familiar with resources in their community as a project goal. They can examine how different organizations, groups, and people collaborate to ensure the well-being of the community and its members. Another goal might involve helping students learn to find ways for participating in the community conversations that matter most to them. We believe in the importance of service hours as a means to create a reciprocal relationship with the community organization. Student research on organizational missions, goals, services, and needs may draw on resources such as organizational artifacts or time spent in an interview. Providing service and new ideas to the organization are ways the student can compensate the organization for their time and resources.

Figure 6.1. Service Learning Partnership Agreement

Student:

I, _____, agree to work during _____ (semester/quarter and year) with _____ (name of organization) for at least _____ hours. I agree to work with my site supervisor to set up a regular schedule and to outline expectations of my service. I agree to bring ideas for further service to the attention of my supervisor. If there are unexpected circumstances and I have to miss a scheduled commitment, I will call ahead of time and let my supervisor know. My site supervisor, to whom I am directly responsible, is _____.

Organization:

_____ (name of organization) agrees to accept _____ (name of student) as a volunteer for _____ hours during _____ (semester/quarter and year). As site supervisor, I agree to provide tasks for him/her to complete while s/he is at the agency. Training necessary for the work s/he is expected to do will be provided. I agree to solicit and discuss other possible service activities that the student may develop. Any change in placement or hours of service will be discussed in advance. I agree that while the student is serving the organization, s/he will not be asked to transport any person, be alone with any minors, or be in any private home without an agency representative on site.

Teacher:

I understand that _____ will volunteer with _____ _____ as part of the requirements for_____ (class), _____semester/quarter _____(year). I agree to provide a framework in which reflection and learning can happen in response to the service experience. I agree to be available for both the student and the site supervisor involved in this contract. I invite and appreciate feedback and evaluation and offer to act as a bridge if there are problems with communication between the student and organization.

Teacher's Contact Information

Name, phone, email: _____

_____

_____   _____
Student signature   Date

_____   _____
Site supervisor signature   Date

_____   _____
Teacher signature   Date

Balancing Student Workload

As we emphasized in Chapter 1, we believe service works best when it is integrated into the curriculum rather than being something extra. In the kind of service to community project that we have described, students' service hours are not extra in the sense that they are being constrained with additional "homework" hours outside of class. When students are asked to perform service outside of regular school hours, we strongly recommend that their service hours get factored into their homework load like any other assignment. This may mean assigning a decreased amount of homework in terms of reading and writing, stretching out the service hours over the course of a semester so students aren't spending more than an hour or so a week at their community sites, or setting aside occasional free time in class to work on an assignment that would normally be completed as homework. In many cases, such work can also be connected to required senior projects.

We also see value in asking students to engage in community service hours outside of school so they learn how service to community can become a regular part of their lives as citizens, even when they have school and work commitments. We can have conversations with students about how service to the greater good often means small (and sometimes big!) sacrifices, and how a lack of convenience and ease does not negate our important roles as mindful democratic citizens.

Reflection on Service Deepens Learning

Reflection and assignments throughout the service project help students make connections between what they have learned and are learning at school, and also help them apply disciplinary knowledge in a real-world context. Some teachers like to have their students complete a preservice reflective writing assignment to explore their choices of community partners, their goals for learning, and any questions they have as they prepare to begin the service experience. Students can revisit their preservice reflective writing after they have completed service hours so they can see what they have learned and consider what they still want to learn, drawing on questions like those in Figure 6.2.

In another possible assignment or in-class exercise, students can consider what the community organization is doing to increase the physical and mental health of the community and the overall well-being of its citizens. Students can also complete short writing assignments in which they make connections with texts they have read for and beyond class, which will provide them with practice integrating various sources into their writing.

Whitney's students write rhetorical analyses of a written artifact such as a brochure or newsletter from the community organization they are serving, in order to examine how writing and rhetoric function outside of academic contexts. The thinking, research, and writing in the community artifact assignment in Figure 6.3

Figure 6.2. Reflection on Challenges and Contributions

At the beginning of the semester, you reflected on which organization you chose for your community partner and why, what you hoped to learn, the strengths and knowledge you brought to the partner, and the initial questions you had. You have now finished serving with your community partner and have learned more about the organization.

Respond to the following questions in writing:

1. How have you been challenged and extended by this experience? If you don't feel you have been challenged and extended, explore the reasons why.
2. What have you learned about yourself, the happiness and well-being of others, and the community as a result?
3. What do you think you have contributed to your community partner? What evidence is there of this contribution? How did your partner contribute to your personal and civic development? What evidence indicates and supports this contribution?
4. How do you imagine yourself being an advocate in your community in the future? What seems most important to you to focus on in terms of the happiness and well-being of your community and its members in the context of your placement? In the context of other possible service organizations or initiatives?
5. What skills do you want to develop and what knowledge do you want to gain to most effectively be the kind of advocate you want to be?

Note to teacher: Regardless of which reflective writing or activities you incorporate, we recommend that you include something that supports students in productively focusing their energy as civic participants. In our experience, students have incredible insights and are excited when they realize their capacity as activists, but they also are easily overwhelmed when they realize the magnitude of social issues and problems that need to be addressed and solved. We find it useful to help them see that they can accomplish more through focused efforts on one or two issues rather than trying to "eat the whole elephant."

builds skills outlined in the Common Core for reading and writing. Teachers can encourage students to share their reflections and findings from an artifact analysis with their community partners, as they can be used for the revision of organizational documents or incorporated into newsletters.

Summative Assessment

After service hours are completed, we recommend inviting students to share their findings with their peers through a culminating project. A culminating project allows students to make visible for themselves and one another what they have learned and what they still want to learn, the challenges they have faced and how they have negotiated those challenges, their contributions, and the strengths they have to offer as community members.

Figure 6.3. Community Artifact Analysis

Students choose a written or multimodal artifact from a community organization to analyze. Consider having students work in small groups to analyze a common artifact for practice before they complete the independent research and writing assignment.

Artifacts might include, but are not limited to, brochures, newsletters, websites, PSAs, sourcebooks, policy documents, volunteer training materials, photography, artwork, multimedia displays, etc.

Listed below are questions to guide students' analyses and to elicit responses grounded in evidence from their artifacts for the claims they make (Common Core Writing Standards 1–2, 7, & 9; Reading Standards 1, 4–7, & 9; Speaking and Listening Standard 3).

1. What do you see? I.e. what is right there (noticing the literal)? What does this make you think (inferring and interpreting)? What does this make you wonder (what questions, evaluations, possible applications arise)?
2. Explore your initial response to the artifact as a member of the community that the organization serves. Does it connect to anything in your experiences, observations, and/or knowledge base? What questions does it raise for you? What might you do to find answers to those questions?
3. What genre/genres is/are the artifact? Which features lead you to believe this? How does this genre(s) help fulfill the purpose of the document? Or not?
4. What modalities are used (text, photos, charts, graphics, hyperlinks, mp3 files, video) and how does this help fulfill the purpose of the document?
5. What is the artifact's purpose? Why was it created? What situations, issues, or questions does it engage? Does it invite, teach, inform, persuade, entertain, encourage reflection, make a call to action, or a combination of these? What features give you these ideas about its purpose?
6. What claim(s), if any, is/are made in this artifact? How is/are the claim(s) supported with evidence? How is reasoning used to connect the evidence to the claim(s), justify the claim(s), and explain how the evidence fits the claim(s)?
7. In what context does this artifact exist or did it grow out of (physically, historically, socially, geographically)? How is the context reflected in the artifact's features?
8. Who is the audience (real or imagined) for this artifact? What implicit beliefs, values, or experiences does the artifact suggest that the audience might share?
9. How does the substance and structure of the artifact work to create specific meanings and effects for the particular audiences to whom it is directed?

For younger students, choose an artifact from an organization such as a local children's museum, theater, or discovery center that is mainly visual, such as a short film or poster. Use the See-Think-Wonder technique (Wilhelm, Wilhelm & Boas, 2008) to prompt them to discuss what they see right there in the document, what each element makes them think (interpret) and wonder about (ask further questions). Have them identify unfamiliar words, phrases, and images and work together to figure out what they might mean based on context clues.

Students can always volunteer not only to provide revision suggestions but to create their own documents to support the organization.

For example, students can collaboratively create a map of the community that documents the work being done by various organizations, groups, and community members to address the happiness and well-being of the community and its members. The map can be an actual map of the community, a directory or web of the various organizations and their bailiwicks, a hyperlinked website or googledoc, and/or it may be an archive of materials that can be passed on to the next class, who can add to and revise the repository as needed. Students can also share the map with their community partners.

With a complete and detailed map of their community organizations and experiences, students can collaboratively consider gaps, silences, and existing needs, raising questions and concerns they have and brainstorming possible ways that they, along with other community members, might begin to address those gaps and needs in ways that will lead to a healthier, happier community. In this way, the current project leads into the future. A final reflective assignment could ask students to consider what the next steps would be for addressing the questions or concerns they have raised, and to brainstorm how they can bring together different organizations or people to address complicated problems. If no community resources yet exist to address particular concerns, students can create plans of action for addressing concerns, in the process seeing how they are activist learners capable of generating possible solutions and tapping into their own networks and resources.

Interdisciplinary Possibilities

In this chapter, we have featured an in-depth community mapping project for middle and high school students that focuses on the following existential question: How does a community work to ensure that its citizens have access to the inalienable rights of life, liberty, and the pursuit of happiness proclaimed in the Declaration of Independence? The values this project espouses are values that can be tapped into for projects on a smaller scale in which students are engaged with service to their communities and are learning to ask questions as democratic citizens who have a responsibility to assume a lifelong inquiry stance and to move from inquiry to action, as each action, no matter how small, is a stone in the pile that leads to change.

This general framework for service to community can also be integrated into various content areas, or can be modified for shorter kinds of piggyback activities that extend the work being done in school. For example, an environmental unit asked the existential question: What is our proper relationship to the environment? As part of this unit, students in various Boise schools helped the Riverkeepers organization clean up the Boise River, another group of Micah Lauer's students became involved in studying and mapping sage grouse and pygmy rabbit habitat. Both groups reflected and wrote about the experience, and became involved with the Idaho Conservation League and the Department of Natural Resources, sharing their data and becoming proactive in planning how to protect habitats.

Jeff's daughter Fiona and her classmates were inspired by a civics unit based on the question, "What is our responsibility to newcomers to our community?" Together, they became involved with the Agency for New Americans and helped refugees tell their stories and articulate their needs. Based on what they had learned through their primary research, Fiona and her peers worked to address the refugees' expressed needs for transportation, integration into the community, and access to health care.

Many students in Boise schools supported and worked for the Special Olympics World Winter Games, hosted in Idaho in 2009, after a unit on achieving equality of opportunity. The unit was framed around the question, "How do we work toward equality for all?" As part of the unit, students worked closely with the visiting competitors as well as local Special Olympics teams. Many students became hosts and mentors for Special Olympians, which turned out to be a transformative experience for them.

Student Understanding

We have found that students often surprise us with the depth of their analysis and understanding of what they contributed as well as the limitations of their contributions. For example, Logan, one of Sara's students, wrote a reflective essay in which he concluded that his service to a local organization that serves at-risk youth and their families had a minimal impact on greater societal issues. Specifically, he and a group of peers spent time helping sort donations of clothing and household goods for the organization's secondhand store. Logan concluded:

> I would venture that helping the [organization] is a beneficial activity for everyone who lives in the area, as a store of any sort provides jobs, goods, and services to the general populace. In a stretch, stronger communities lead to stronger education systems, which provide more teachers and more advanced subjects that can be taught to students. If the idea is pulled paper thin, my education allows me the opportunity to help an organization that may have helped my community elevate me to the place I am at today. And that, I suppose, is a form of justice. The service was indirect in nature, so we did not actually address any societal issues or change the community for the better. We were simply helping out.

His recognition of the limits of this particular form of service gave us hope for his future. Falling somewhere between Morton's (2010) charity and project levels of service, Logan recognized that his service did not contribute directly to social change or address deeper issues. Combine that recognition with support and opportunities to engage in social change, and this student will be on his way to engaging in service to community that can *transform* community.

WRITING AND SPEAKING TO ADVOCATE

In situations or locales where serving with community organizations is not ideal or possible, students can still attend to community issues and learn how to intervene in cultural conversations. Writing or speaking to advocate provides students with an opportunity to write for real rather than imagined audiences, and to learn how writing does multiple kinds of work in the world. Students frequently make more conscious rhetorical choices because the stakes are not just grades but also their identities and the functional work they wish to achieve because their writing or speaking is going public.

Tapping into their interest inventories, students can choose issues that matter to them to research further in order to compose outreach plans, presentations for the community, photography and other kinds of documentary exhibits, or advocacy pieces such as op/eds or public service announcements. We encourage students to work collaboratively with others who share their interests. For example, students may want to organize an outreach effort that they can carry out together to ensure that there is a support system for speaking to community members for what may be the first time. The outreach advocacy guide in Figure 6.4, adapted from Rinku Sen's (2003) *Stir It Up: Lessons in Community Organizing and Advocacy*, can be used to help students frame an outreach endeavor.

Family and community members can be invited to class to provide students with practice in presenting their ideas to a live audience and getting feedback before they engage in the community. Even if students are unable to engage in the actual outreach, through the planning and research process, they acquire skills and habits of mind that position them to do such work in the future.

Students who write or speak to advocate draw on the same CCSS and habits of mind that are cultivated through the aforementioned mapping the community project. Even if they do not complete service hours with a community organization, they can still compose rhetorical analyses of brochures, websites, and other readily available artifacts from community organizations. After students analyze how an artifact's features reflect a particular audience, purpose, and context, they can (re)create the artifact for a different audience. This type of radical revision would require additional research to meet the needs of the new audience. For example, perhaps the original artifact included short, powerful narratives about the population the organization served as a way of appealing to the emotions of community members. The radically revised artifact might target large businesses, whose presidents might value statistics more than stories, and thus would call on the student to find a new set of data for effective advocacy.

Students also experience activist learning when they conduct independent research and design their own advocacy pieces based on their careful consideration of their research, audience, and purposes for advocacy, as the project in

Figure 6.4. Outreach Advocacy Guide

Developing an Issue to Pursue (Common Core Writing Standards 7–9)

1. Conduct research *before* engaging in outreach. Write down questions that arise or challenging and provocative comments you hear and conduct additional research *throughout* the process.
2. What values, beliefs, and assumptions do you (or your group, if the project is collaborative) carry into your community outreach?
3. What values, beliefs, and assumptions do others hold that you need to take into consideration in order to be most effective as a/an advocate(s)?
4. What initial ideas do you have to raise awareness about the issue and/or invite others into the conversation or work with you on behalf of this issue?

Questions to Think About when Planning
(Common Core Speaking and Listening Standards 1–2)

1. What is the issue? Can you explain it concisely and with clarity?
2. What demands do you face in addressing the issue, and do you have someone who can inform you or assist you in meeting those demands?
3. Who is the target audience, where is the target audience located, and why do you think the target audience can help address the issue?
4. What is your larger message? If someone asked, in reference to your issue, "So what?" how would you answer?
5. What is the plan for action? Can your planned action draw the media to increase visibility of the issue? How can you archive materials so that attention can be paid over time?
6. What groups and organizations might be good allies? What contributions might they make?
7. What roles will you assign (e.g., people to testify, a media spokesperson, and so forth), and how do those roles draw on participants' knowledge and abilities?
8. What could go wrong? What obstacles may come up? Is your plan flexible enough to shift if necessary?

Reflection After Implementing Plan (SL 4–6)

1. Did you carry out your plan in its entirety? What actually happened?
2. What was unexpected and surprising?
3. What worked? Kind of worked? Did not work? How do you know?
4. What were the principles of action that explain what worked or did not work? How can you use these principles to revise future actions?
5. How can your experience help you plan for future activist efforts?

Online Figure I illustrates. Whichever approach to advocacy students take, they should be encouraged to seek venues for making their writing public or published so they can experience firsthand the work that their writing and speaking can do for good in the world.

DEVELOPING CARING CITIZENS

K–12 students have tremendous power to address social needs and enact change in their communities, because they come at issues and problems from fresh perspectives and with the energy of youth. We have observed how, when students see their capacity for serving their communities, they continue to seek new community service opportunities. For example, one of Whitney's students, a waitress at a local restaurant, started a recycling project after noticing that the restaurants that lined the street where she worked were throwing out large numbers of bottles each night because there was no curbside recycling. She asked business owners if they would mind saving those bottles and putting them in the alley behind their restaurants so she or one of her friends could come pick them up and take them to a recycling station each night.

If we help students recognize themselves as a critical part of their communities and foster skills and habits of mind for advocacy while they are young, we are preparing our students for their future responsibility as full participants in democracy as voters but even more as citizens who care about the community and about developing its resources and meeting its needs.

CHAPTER 7

Service to the Environment and Global Community

Building Skills and Habits of Mind to Transform Our World

Rose Beal is a Holocaust survivor and human rights activist who lives in Boise, Idaho. Rose managed to escape Nazi Germany and come to the United States in 1939. She recalls her overwhelming feelings of hope and relief when her ship arrived in the New York harbor and she first saw the Statue of Liberty. Despite only having the equivalent of $2.50 in U.S. dollars to help her begin life anew, Rose proceeded to make her way in freedom and lived the American Dream. For Rose, the American Dream was more than having a successful career and raising her children; it meant being a human rights activist. As she said, "How could anyone survive what I did and not become a human rights activist?"

Todd DeStigter (2001) described democracy as "a process of associated living in which individuals participate in deciding what their world should be like, in acting to pursue these aims, and in sharing equitably in the consequences of that action" (p. 12). A living example of DeStigter's words in action, Rose decided long ago that the world should not include tyranny, persecution, and genocide. Even in her 90s, she continues to pursue those aims by being an active volunteer with the Wassmuth Center for Human Rights in Idaho.

Rose's contributions to human rights often involve speaking to groups of students. Her words always have a poignant effect, and have even helped inspire a youth human rights movement for middle school students in Boise, which we will explore in detail in this chapter. In conversations with students, Rose points out the problem with rhetoric. Lots of people say we should study the Holocaust so we don't forget and don't let genocide happen again. Yet, as Rose says, "Never again is obsolete. Never again is now." She points out that there are contemporary genocides and many human rights violations happening at this very second. Rose's words challenge us all to respond to the moral imperative of standing up when confronted by injustice, and of working proactively to (re)shape our world into a place where human rights are honored and upheld. It's far easier to do nothing, or to hope others will address problems. Rose reminds us not to let ourselves off the hook; we are part of a shared humanity, and we must all take responsibility for our world.

93

As we have shown throughout this book, service learning creates opportunities for students—and their teachers—to contribute to (re)shaping our world. Through service to our environment and global community, we can help children and adolescents have experiences that empower them with the knowledge that they can contribute to bettering our world. In the sections that follow, we offer five inspiring examples of service to the environment and/or global community to illustrate the myriad possibilities.

YOUTH FOR HUMAN RIGHTS:
SERVICE TO THE GLOBAL COMMUNITY

Middle school teacher Diane Williams—a National Writing Project fellow, Holocaust Educators Network member, and the 2011 Idaho Human Rights Educator of the Year—recounts a memorable classroom moment. Through the inquiry-orientated discussion technique called Socratic Seminar, Diane's students were discussing whether World War II and its horrors could have been avoided. One of her students loudly blurted out, "This pisses me off!" Diane was not used to that kind of language in her class, but she took a deep breath because she knew something bigger was at stake. She reframed her student's exclamation as a question: "What is it that makes you so mad?" Her student responded:

> You told us learning about the Holocaust is important, because it's our
> generation's responsibility to bear witness to the past so that such atrocities
> never happen again. But look around. Last year we studied Africa and learned
> about Darfur. Remember what Rose Beal told us when we were studying the
> Holocaust? "Never again is obsolete. Never again is now." We have to carry
> these images of genocide and the Holocaust in our heads and hearts forever.
> The world never seems to learn from its past, and it pisses me off.

Diane remembers the silence that greeted the student's passionate explanation, giving her a moment to collect her thoughts before responding with the most important question of her teaching career: "What would you like to do about it?" The silence was shattered as her students exploded with ideas, and soon broke into small groups to brainstorm actionable ways they could raise awareness about human rights violations.

By responding with an invitation to take action, Diane gave her students the opportunity to develop what can be described as "democratic character." John Goodlad (2000) explained that the mission of schools must include "the enculturation of the young into the freedoms and responsibilities of a democratic society" (p. 86). Diane's students enacted Goodlad's words by identifying actions that they would like to take that reflected their growing understanding of their responsibilities as citizens in a democratic society. Having knowledge and not *doing* something meaningful with it was not acceptable to her middle school students—a stance we want all students to have for life. With Diane's guidance, her students created the first annual Youth for Human Rights Celebration.

For 5 consecutive years, Diane's students have held the daylong celebration in the spring. It is staged at a public memorial in a part of downtown Boise that gets a lot of foot traffic, creating opportunities for invited guests and passersby to stop and take part in the event. The celebration provides Diane's students with opportunities to educate others and to advocate for political and humanitarian action; students perform literary pieces that they have developed through research about human rights. The process includes reading a variety of informational texts, reflective writing and talking, and an in-depth revision and peer feedback process—all skills outlined in the CCSS.

When they are not performing their literary works, students interact with attendees and invite them to visit their Universal Declaration of Human Rights exhibits. Diane gives each student the responsibility of becoming an expert on one of the 30 articles in the Declaration. Students research contemporary examples of human rights violations of as well as efforts to protect "their" right. Through a research and rhetorical decisionmaking process similar to the Community Artifact Analysis process we described in Chapter 6, students become curators, making exhibits that invite their audience to engage in activist conversations with them. Diane explained:

> Their objective is to raise awareness about human rights. I have encouraged them to be advocates of truth, looking at the gray areas where truths meet rather than to take a hard political stance. By the very nature of what they are doing, they are engaging in democracy because they are involved in the conversation.

The opportunity to share their expertise validates the extensive time students devote to preparing for the celebration.

Although the celebration has been a successful and popular student choice for years, Diane values student buy-in and does not require future students to stage the event. She is open to other possibilities that her next generation of students may identify as a way to make their learning of service. She has embraced an approach to teaching in which she is helping the students to do their own chosen work.

The celebration was the result of Diane listening to students, her own dynamic mindset as a teacher, a willingness to embrace challenges, and the underlying belief that her students have the ability to do something meaningful. Especially powerful was the way in which the student who inspired the celebration was given an opportunity to express her opinion and have it heard through

Socratic Seminar. We encourage teachers to use techniques like Socratic Seminar as ways to include opportunities for democratic dialogue in conjunction with service learning inquiry-based units.

SERVICE TO THE LOCAL COMMUNITY THAT CAN GO GLOBAL

This past year, Jeff was approached by the school at a local St. Luke's children's hospital about writing curriculum for hospital bound and homebound school-age students. Upon exploration, he found that there was no curriculum designed for such students, and he approached his Boise State Writing Project Leadership team about beginning this project by creating a curriculum around composing autobiographies, organized around the existential question, "How do people respond to the 'trouble'/challenges they face?"

The hospital teachers endorsed this idea, confirming that many students found therapeutic value in telling their stories of struggle, whether they wished to explore the challenges of their illness or something else. Many of the students are terminal, and want to provide an archival memento and gift to their families.

The following was agreed upon as a rationale for the action plan:

Rationale:
Narrative is in the Common Core State Standards (and Idaho Core) and therefore in all curricula in the state of Idaho at all grade levels. Narrative is "natural" and "the primary mode of mind" according to brain researcher Barbara Hardy. Learning to compose narrative through autobiography will provide transfer value to the reading and writing of a wide variety of narratives. Narrative is also the emphasis of the Idaho State Department of Education's work with teachers during this coming school year, and this will give us a chance to provide assistance to the teachers and students at St. Luke's in this regard.

Personal autobiographical narratives are "close to home" since all students have experiences they can write about. Such writing has the potential to lead to personal growth since it allows one to consider and reflect on personal experience and the meaning of it. Such writing also has the potential to provide therapeutic value because writing can help one make personal connections, connections to others, and to promote a dynamic mindset regarding one's capacity to face challenges. Personal stories are important to individuals and can bridge to issues of cultural importance.

We will compose differentiated curriculum that can be scaled up and down to meet needs of K–12 students. The curriculum will consist of one hour modules that will explore big moves like noticing characterization as readers and creating it as writers; plot moves like setting up trouble and dealing with it; conventional moves like incorporating quotes or using apostrophes with possession. The goal is to give students transferable tools that will help them compose their autobiography but that are transferable to other iterations of composing and reading narrative and that also tie to CCSS and most school curricula—and that can easily be tweaked to do so more closely in the cases of individual students.

Furthermore, it was decided that a core group of teachers would develop central modules for a semester-long curriculum that could be differentiated for use from kindergarten through the 12th grade and that would connect to various other modules that could extend each of the core modules. Teachers developed the curriculum with their students, and then field tested it with the students. In this way, the BSWP teachers' students provided the service of co-developing the curriculum. (This provided a side benefit as these students considered how to serve and stay connected to fellow students who missed long periods of school for any reason, and how to reacclimate those long absent to school upon their return.)

Next, the modules were sent to the local hospital for use. The hospital students there also provided service by reflecting on their use of the materials, so the modules could be revised before dissemination to other hospitals across the country and world. Currently, the students in the schools and hospital are planning online writing groups so that they can be of service to each other as writers. They are also conferring as they plan the next units of study they would like to help develop for use in the local hospital, as well as for hospital schools across the country and globe.

SERVICE TO THE ENVIRONMENT
FOR EMERGING READERS AND WRITERS

At Anser Charter School in Boise, teachers guide students in learning expeditions that involve in-depth inquiry into a topic spanning a semester or longer. For kindergarten students, birds provide an accessible and engaging expedition topic. Teacher Anne Moore explained that her students are "so full of wonderment. They are already familiar with birds, so it is a real and authentic topic that they can grab onto right away." Influenced by the Reggio Emilia approach to early childhood education, Anne believes that when children are young they should be taught to love and value nature—then they can be taught to savor and save it. By exploring the developmentally appropriate inquiry questions "What makes a bird a bird? Why protect birds?" her students have opportunities to:

> Learn bird identification skills and discover the habits, needs and joys of birds, not only in their backyard, but in other parts of the world, too. Through habitat improvement, research, and service, kindergartners learn about the natural world, the fragile existence of wildlife and the need to be caretakers of living things. (Bird Exploration, 2012, para. 1)

They also learn basic and substantive skills of science and of composing, and develop an understanding of informational text structures featured in the CCSS: definition, grouping, differentiating and classifying, basic research skills such as observation and note-taking, nature drawing, noticing key details, seeing relationships such as cause and effect, and much more. They also learn about birds, ecosystems, habitats, symbiosis, and other conceptual knowledge.

One of the culminating service events for the unit involves sharing the results of the students' inquiry by providing service to a local nature center. Each kindergartner contributes to a showcase of knowledge about local birds, sharing the results of their inquiry into one specific species. The students sell notecards featuring detailed drawings of their bird, and the money raised goes to the nonprofit nature center dedicated to environmental stewardship.

To produce notecard-worthy drawings, students complete an in-depth revision process that allows them to develop their drawing skills and the ability to self-assess their work and act upon constructive feedback from others. (See Figure 7.1 for an example of a Northern Flicker notecard that a student named Henry Seely created.) The knowledge artifacts created by the students become archival and are a form of service to the future. These are impressive accomplishments for young learners who are developing foundational reading and writing skills. Anne explained, "Writing and reading is difficult at this age. But because they're so excited about birds, reading and writing becomes really motivating for them because of the importance of their learning."

Looking back on his kindergarten learning experience in Anne's classroom, 10-year-old Henry Seely reflected, "It's very dear to me because it was my first expedition. I thought it was pretty good to know about birds. It still comes in handy when I'm in the woods; I can help people identify birds." Henry also noted how his knowledge promotes an understanding of how environmental resources and pressures affect ecosystems and the birds within them.

Henry continues to be a naturalist concerned about issues in his environment, and he shows an ever-emerging understanding of the importance of conservation at the local and global levels. Henry's words reflect the essence of what Nagel and Beauboeuf (2012) explained: Young learners can begin to understand "the concept of caring for our Earth, and develop a sense of global responsibility and community . . . [and] recognize their power as citizens of a global community" (p. 7). Early inquiry experiences like the bird expedition that combine service with in-depth learning leave lasting and empowering memories for young learners, laying the groundwork for the habits of mind they need to become activist citizens.

COMBINING GLOBAL AND ENVIRONMENTAL SERVICE

Teachers can design inquiry with service to the local environment as an outcome *and* guide students to make connections to larger global situations. For example,

Figure 7.1. Northern Flicker Notecard

Northern Flicker

The Flicker gets pushed out of its nest by small mammals and other birds. It eats ants, beetles larvae, fruit, nuts and seeds. The males' wingspan is 20 inches and 18 for the female and it's 12-14 inches long. Its nest is a tree cavity and it lays 6-8 white eggs. It has a reddish orangish on its wing and on its tail and on its cheek. It has light tan white on its wings and its belly with black spots. It has a black breast patch and it has gray chiseling beak. It has gray climbing feet and it sounds like "wicka, wicka, wicka" when it is talking to its mate and it beats its beak on a pole when it is attracting a mate.

By: HENRY   Research Buddy: Logan

These cards were created by Kindergarten students from the ANSER Charter School, a public school in Boise, Idaho. They reflect the children's yearlong study of birds. All proceeds from the sale of these cards will go toward bird conservation and rehabilitation efforts in Idaho.

ANSER Charter School: An Expeditionary Learning Center

our colleague Jill Hettinger has taught high school science and served as a K–8 science specialist. Jill offered a remarkable elective science, technology, engineering, and math (STEM) service learning course with service opportunities that centered on community needs. In-class content centered on developing a deep understanding of the three pillars of sustainable development: economic, societal, and environmental. Sustainable development offers economic and societal growth *and* environmental protection.

By considering the ramifications of different options to protect environmental resources with regard to each pillar, students began to understand the complexity of decisionmaking. Finding solutions that honor the needs or goals represented by each pillar is difficult. Rather than try to become an expert in all three areas, Jill invited a series of guest speakers to address each pillar and the related issues. She reflected, "There is no way any one teacher can have a rich depth of knowledge in all three areas—but an expert can!" This approach allowed her to be a model learner; instead of adopting the typical teacher-as-expert role, Jill enhanced her own knowledge along with that of her students.

When teaching with service learning in this way, a teacher like Jill embraces a paradigm shift for her role in the class. Rather than teachers needing to conceive of themselves as the lone experts in the classroom and the purveyor of information, teachers embrace the role of co-learner, co-inquirer, and collaborator with their students in creating knowledge, culture, and service. This act allows teachers to model learning-centered sociocultural teaching, as well as democratic citizenship by positioning themselves as learners and inquirers.

Jill's students used two case studies to understand economic, societal, and environmental sustainability. One case study was local, and it involved the service experience of monitoring wood duck boxes for Idaho Fish and Game at a local lake near Boise. Students also reviewed policy documents that reflected all three pillars of sustainability for dam building. These sources provided authentic informational text reading and analysis experiences called for in the CCSS. The document analysis made it clear to students how difficult it can be to make decisions that meet all stakeholders' needs.

The second case study was international; students read Bruce Barcott's (2008) book *The Last Flight of the Scarlet Macaw: One Woman's Fight to Save the World's Most Beautiful Bird*. Situated in Belize, Barcott's book tells the story of Sharon Matola's efforts to stop the Belizean government from building a controversial dam that ruined thousands of acres of wildlife habitat, including nesting grounds for an imperiled population of scarlet macaws. The book provides a heart-wrenching example of the interplay among the three pillars of sustainability: Inaccurate information about the potential economic and societal gains triumphed over environmental concerns.

By comparing the issues in Belize with the monitoring of the local wood duck population, Jill's students learned that the issues were similar despite the fact that they occurred in different parts of the world. Idaho Fish and Game built wood duck boxes after dams wiped out this species' natural nesting places: tree cavities.

Rather than go in-depth with service to one community organization, Jill identified an array of six service opportunities in her community that were relevant to STEM during the semester in which she taught the course. These were stand-alone, one-time service opportunities, and students participated in two options. This flexibility allowed students to have a choice in what they did and also enabled them to pick the events that worked best with their schedules. The service opportunities all took place outside of regular school hours.

One option involved serving with Idaho Fish and Game on a wood duck counting event and asking questions such as, "What are the environmental effects of dam building? What happens when a species' natural habitat is destroyed?" Another option was helping with a habitat restoration day in the Boise foothills, with inquiries such as, "How can we prevent erosion? How do forest and wildland fires affect an ecosystem? How can we restore native ecosystems?" Other students cotaught a community education course about wind energy for upper elementary and middle-level students, asking questions such as, "How can we live sustainably? How can we meet our energy needs?"

Jill found the experience of teaching the course incredibly rewarding. Although we may not be able to teach an elective class like Jill's, her approach illustrates generalizable possibilities:

1. Identify community needs and use one or more to create a service
   learning experience that connects to the curriculum already being taught.

2. Consider offering students a small "menu" of service experiences in which they can participate outside of school to enhance their in-school learning. Challenge students to add to the menu. Consider including service experiences that students can participate in with their families in order to strengthen school-home connections.

3. Study a local issue that reflects a community need and give it global relevance by using a case study from another part of the world. From poverty to environmental degradation, there is no shortage of issues that have international parallels.

Multiple global or environmental service learning projects can arise from addressing community needs (see **Online Figure J**). We mention a couple here to illustrate the extensive possibilities. Boise is one of the refugee centers of North America. We have already described how many students in local schools have provided various services to refugee populations. Our colleague Michal Temkin-Martinez, a linguistics professor, additionally engages students in recording and preserving native languages from our refugee populations that are in danger of dying out, and in some cases, creating written versions of languages that are only oral. Michal's project provides a service to the global community as students simultaneously address a local need in their community.

Boise is in the high desert, and many teachers have created units of instruction and service around habitat protection, as we've seen with Jill's project. Teachers have also developed units that address issues of water use and preservation, public use of lands, and other issues of local importance. What are the environmental and/or humanitarian needs in your community?

SERVING OUR COMMUNITIES AND BEYOND: INTERNATIONAL GLOBAL SERVICE

Since 2010 Sara has been part of the Belize Education Project (BEP), a small, teacher-led, nonprofit organization based in Colorado, made up of a group of educators who have taken their passion for literacy and commitment to active citizenship to a global level by making a long-term commitment to improve literacy and education in the Cayo District of Belize, Central America. The vision developed in 2007 when 1st-grade teacher Jean Kirshner accompanied a surgical mission trip to Belize. The medical team arranged for her to help at a school in the town of Santa Elena, so Jean filled her luggage with books and set off to read with children. When she shared the story of a school filled with beautiful children who were eager to learn to read and teachers with love in their hearts but limited resources and pedagogical training, medical professionals realized that Belizeans wouldn't reach the point of being able to perform their own surgeries or even monitor their own health care without more advanced levels of literacy.

Wanting to contribute to Belize in a way that would help build an entire community, Rebecca Knight, a surgeon, and Chris Robinson, a nurse, joined Jean in creating a professional development program to help lift children's lives through literacy. Reflecting on her first visit to a school in Santa Elena, Chris said, "We had a choice to make: We could do something, or we could do nothing." Guided by a mantra similar to the one Rose Beal underscores when she reminds us that "never again is now," Chris, Rebecca, and Jean responded to the moral imperative of doing something (see Figure 7.2) and acted when they were confronted by global educational disparity and poverty. Their action led to a lasting professional development model that provides teachers and students in the United States and Belize with powerful service learning opportunities.

Each October, BEP teachers from Colorado (plus Sara from Idaho) travel to Belize for a week to work with students and provide professional development for up to 40 teachers at three schools in the Cayo District. The BEP also brings Belizean educators to the United States for professional development each April. Over the years, close friendships have developed between teachers in both countries, and the long-term relationship allows them to see the students grow up and become readers. Those relationships form the heart of the BEP. As Jean explained,

> We know from teaching that authentic change really only happens within a relationship. You can add an alphabet song, give a trick of one, two, three—eyes on me, but philosophical changes—paradigm shifts—only happen within the context of relationships. (Fry, 2012, p. 77)

The results of these relationships create lasting, personal connections that make transformation possible.

Inviting U.S. students to join in the mission of lifting lives through literacy was a natural extension of the BEP; the students' participation helps make the initiative sustainable. Because most of the BEP teachers work in the same school district in Colorado, it has become commonplace for their students to engage in a variety of age-appropriate service learning projects throughout their elementary school years.

Primary Students' Service Learning and Inquiry About Belize

At the beginning of each school year, Jean Kirshner's 1st-grade students begin the journey to global citizenship by studying Belize. They learn about its culture, climate, and place on the globe, which provides rich opportunities for the students to develop skills and knowledge outlined by the National Council for the Social Studies (2010), such as understanding global connections and interdependence. Then, to personalize their understanding so that Belize becomes more than just a place on map, Jean's students, as she notes, "write letters to students far away from

Figure 7.2. On Doing Something or Doing Nothing

We are often confronted by the opportunity to do something or walk away, having done nothing. Providing students with service learning experiences at a young age can help them develop the habits of mind that lead to activist citizenship. We are reminded of the popular motivational story adapted from Loren Eiseley's (1978) essay and book *The Star Thrower:*

While walking along a beach, an old man noticed a boy bending down to pick up an object and throwing it into the sea. When the old man asked the boy what he is doing, the youth responded, "Throwing starfish into the ocean. The tide has washed them up onto the beach and they can't return to the sea by themselves. When the sun gets high, they will die, unless I throw them back into the water." The old man replied, "But there must be tens of thousands of starfish on this beach. I'm afraid you won't really be able to make much of a difference." The boy bent down, picked up yet another starfish and threw it as far as he could into the ocean. Then he turned, smiled, and said, "It made a difference to that one!"

This motivational story can be used to inspire youth to understand the potential they have to make a difference in the world. Even if their initial efforts are small in comparison to global humanitarian and environmental needs, small actions can lead to more actions and to positive outcomes for those who are directly involved.

us in location, but so near us in their passion to become literate." Through discussion, questioning, writing, and conversations about Belizean experiences, Jean's students develop literacy skills outlined in the CCSS.

As their study of Belize continues, the 1st-graders learn about the disparity of resources between their school in Colorado and the school their Belizean pen pals attend. The opportunity allows these young learners to begin developing an understanding of production, distribution, and consumption, which the National Council for the Social Studies (2010) highlights in its thematic curriculum standards. Concerned about their distant friends' lack of access to seemingly basic school supplies that children in the United States often take for granted, the 1st-graders decide to help collect school supplies for their peers in learning.

Although Jean intentionally guides her students to this point, she doesn't tell them that they need to collect school supplies. Instead, she helps them identify the need and to recognize an action they can take. She emphasizes to her students, "Although we may be more resource rich, we are all rich in our ability to learn." Jean is intentional in her approach—she does not want her young learners to develop stereotypes about Americans needing to save people in developing nations through charity. Rather, she approaches the study of Belize and efforts to provide support as an act of solidarity in the quest for literacy. Her students demonstrate an emerging understanding of how the supplies and books they send can help fight illiteracy. Jean frames her approach under the existential question: What issues confront and unite children around the world?

Because the majority of Colorado students involved in the BEP live in fairly affluent suburban communities, their opportunity for a high-quality education is a given, as is having enough food to eat every day. This is not the case for the Belizean students, and the personal insights and connections that unfold through this shared journey to literacy help U.S. students develop a better understanding of their own privileges. Jean explained, "My students did not ask to be born affluent or to live in communities filled with resources. We feel a tremendous responsibility to teach them to be critical thinkers; good stewards of all they will have; and compassionate, informed global citizens." Through their cultural exchange, writing, and photos, Belizean students play a vital role in teaching their long-distance counterparts in Colorado the importance of embracing their responsibilities as citizens, fostering a reciprocal relationship between Belize and U.S. citizens.

Colorado students continue to study Belize in the spring when Belizean teachers come to Colorado for professional development. Jean's 1st-graders interview the teachers about their students and their way of life. The visiting teachers tell the students about Belize and share stories of their students' dreams and hopes. These conversations help the Colorado students appreciate Belizean students' ingenuity and develop an understanding of the basic issues and concerns that unite them despite different life circumstances. Ultimately, students have a year-long experience in which they learn about Belizean culture and act in solidarity with their long-distance friends and partners in learning, striving toward the same goal: literacy.

Meaningful early experiences help young learners embark on the journey toward active global citizenship and an understanding of how they are interconnected with children in another part of the world. The BEP teachers' intentional efforts to promote students' understanding of similarities and connections plant seeds that contribute to Ellen Cushman's (1996) call to erode traditional power structures by aiming to forge interdependency among people.

Intermediate Students' Service Learning

The connection to Belizean partners in learning does not end after 1st grade. The conversations become more sophisticated as children grow older and gain more experience learning about Belize. For example, Shari Griffin's 4th-graders tackled the complicated National Council for the Social Studies' (2010) thematic standard of production, distribution, and consumption as they analyzed the disparity of resources between Belizean schools and their own school. They were surprised to learn that crayons cost five times more in Belize than in the United States, and noted that because pencils, pens, and paper were consumable resources, there was a constant need for those supplies. The 4th-graders found it unacceptable that a scarcity of resources might prevent a student from becoming literate and were determined to help. The class worked with the student council to plan a fundraiser. The result was a successful schoolwide wear-a-hat event that raised money to purchase school supplies for their long-distance partners in learning.

By sharing their love of literacy and close connections with Belizeans with their U.S. students, the BEP teachers enhance the already rewarding nature of their work. Their students develop habits of mind to *identify issues* and *initiate action*, and they learn what is necessary to actually pursue that action. This dynamism is in contrast to merely receiving information. Because of their understanding of issues, they go beyond Morton's (2010) charity level of citizen action and approach social change.

For example, by the time Shari's former 4th-grade students reached 6th grade, they wanted to do more than just donate school supplies and decided to raise money to provide scholarships for two Belizean students to attend high school. Secondary school fees are approximately $650 a year, and this expense is prohibitive for many families. The intrepid 6th-graders raised $1,120 through a 3-day bake sale to provide scholarships and school supplies. The students saw themselves as active participants in the endeavor to meet the BEP's mission statement: "lifting lives through literacy." The bake sale and the supply drives were not one-time fundraising events; rather, they were part of a larger, sustainable endeavor connected to the literacy and citizenship skills that students were learning through curriculum.

As global citizens, the bake-sale students were not marketing their products, but were promoting the importance of education and literacy for students in Belize. Students from all grade levels purchased homemade goods, and instead of asking for change back, they told the 6th-graders to keep the change and asked how close they were to their goal. The 6th-graders recognized that their decisions and actions had extended outward to affect those around them.

For these students, the BEP is not merely a 1-week trip that their teachers take in October or a visit from Belizean teachers in April. Students' contributions also sustain the BEP mission and provide a sense of joy and rejuvenation for their teachers; with 6 months between face-to-face visits with Belizean colleagues, having a community of Colorado students and families who care about the BEP is uplifting. Figure 7.3 depicts this reciprocal relationship. (This section was adapted from a 2012 article by Fry, Griffin, and Kirshner.)

DEVELOPING A GLOBAL SERVICE LEARNING PROJECT

Any teacher can create opportunities for students to develop an understanding of the world and develop the disposition, skills, and desire to take action through a long-term global service learning project (GSL) by partnering with a school or students in a developing nation. In Figures 7.4, 7.5, and 7.6 we offer suggestions to help get started. There is no set entry point to begin developing a GSL; we have found the process iterative.

Figure 7.3. Reciprocity in Action

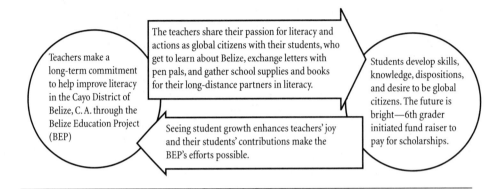

Teachers make a long-term commitment to help improve literacy in the Cayo District of Belize, C. A. through the Belize Education Project (BEP)

The teachers share their passion for literacy and actions as global citizens with their students, who get to learn about Belize, exchange letters with pen pals, and gather school supplies and books for their long-distance partners in literacy.

Seeing student growth enhances teachers' joy and their students' contributions make the BEP's efforts possible.

Students develop skills, knowledge, dispositions, and desire to be global citizens. The future is bright—6th grader initiated fund raiser to pay for scholarships.

Figure 7.4. Possible Inquiry Questions to Explore Through a Global Service Learning Project

- What is service for? Who does it benefit?
- What is literacy for? How can we use literacy to be of service?
- What support/nurturing/assistance is required for success, literacy, self-empowerment?

Figure 7.5. Connecting with Students and Schools in Developing Nations

There are many nonprofit organizations that provide support to children in developing nations. Some of these organizations have the infrastructure to help teachers connect with students and/or schools and facilitate the development of a relationship. For example, the Belize Education Project can facilitate sponsorship of individual secondary-level students; school fees cost approximately $650 a year and are more than many families can afford. You can learn more about the BEP at www.belizeeducationproject.com/index.html.

There are dozens, perhaps hundreds, of other nonprofits that promote education in developing nations that you can also contact. We have direct knowledge of how one such organization has helped American educators and/or students have transformative learning experiences while helping youth in developing nations: Make a Difference (MAD) supports quality educational opportunities for vulnerable children and youth in Tanzania and India. MAD endeavors to help children rise out of poverty and become leaders within their communities. Donors can sponsor an individual child by helping to pay for their school tuition, boarding, and school uniforms.

> Website: http://www.gomadnow.org/madsite
> Email: info@MakeADifferenceNOW.org

In addition to these two organizations with which we are familiar, Half the Sky (www.halftheskymovement.org/partners) offers information about more than 30 nonprofits, including organizations such as Heifer International that offer curriculum resources for service learning. Learn more at www.heifer.org/.

Figure 7.6. Developing a Global Service Learning (GSL) Project

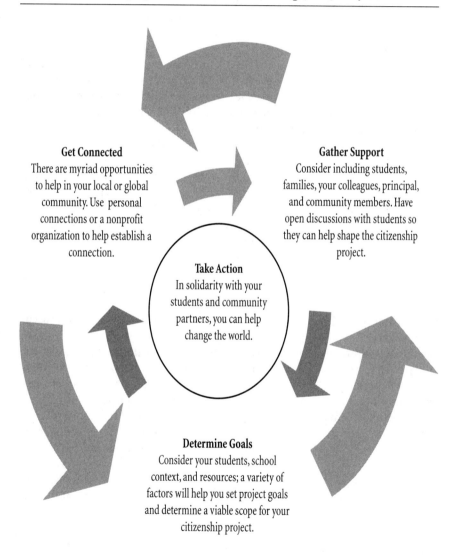

Get Connected
There are myriad opportunities to help in your local or global community. Use personal connections or a nonprofit organization to help establish a connection.

Gather Support
Consider including students, families, your colleagues, principal, and community members. Have open discussions with students so they can help shape the citizenship project.

Take Action
In solidarity with your students and community partners, you can help change the world.

Determine Goals
Consider your students, school context, and resources; a variety of factors will help you set project goals and determine a viable scope for your citizenship project.

As more people in a community take on roles as global citizens, they can help shape a GSL based on their talents and resources. We have found it more effective to have a specific focus for the service—for example, improved literacy instruction for Belizean students as the goal, with professional development for teachers as the mechanism for achieving that goal. It may be easier yet no less powerful to start small for a GSL. For example, if most students in a school come from low-income homes and fundraising might be difficult, a teacher can look into providing a scholarship for one student's school fees instead of trying to take on a partnership with an entire school.

Offering a service that does not require financial resources, such as providing moral support and ideas through a pen pal project, is another option. Students can take pride in their contributions, learn about another student through letter exchanges (which can be facilitated by email to avoid the time and expense of international postage), and share and learn about issues in the pen pal's country.

Regardless of the GSL that a teacher, students, and community develop, they will participate in a meaningful learning adventure as global citizens who take action. We encourage teachers to cultivate a culture in which students view the child or children in another nation as their partner(s) in learning rather than as people who need Americans to "save" them through charity. Most important of all, we open the inquiry to students by asking, "What do you think we should do to help?" Their suggestions may be the start of new solutions.

GLOBAL DISPOSITIONS

In this chapter, we have explored a variety of ways in which teachers can engage their students in learning that provides a service to the environment, the local/global community, or both. Meaningful service learning of this nature can help students learn to embrace Jeff and Sarah Veigel's mantra: Don't let yourself off the hook! We all have a moral imperative to stand up to injustice, to help (re)shape our world into a place where human rights are upheld, and to protect and preserve our environment. We all must be citizens who take ethical action, and providing service to the environment and global community can help children and adolescents develop the disposition and sense of agency to continue to do so in adulthood.

We have found that students are eager to learn in ways that matter and to contribute to solving problems. Diane Williams shared her thoughts on the importance of providing service learning experiences:

> Teaching the "what" is not enough. If you want to fully engage students, there has to be a "so what," something that connects *their* world to *the* world. Inquiry-based curriculum inspires students to think critically and independently, and to act for the good at all. Despite rumors, teens are not as

self-absorbed as one may think. Given the chance, they find great satisfaction and fulfillment in the act of learning and of service. My job is to create ways for their voices to be heard and valued in the classroom, in the school and in the greater community.

We remind ourselves that our students may have many ideas to address and may be able to make progress toward solving the problems that overwhelm us as adults.

Thirty years after she escaped Nazi Germany, Holocaust survivor Rose Beal had the opportunity to visit her former elementary school teacher. Like Rose, her teacher was Jewish and had managed to avoid being murdered by the Nazis. After catching up about their lives and accomplishments, the teacher asked Rose if she still remembered her Latin verbs. Rose confessed that she did not. Her teacher laughed and assured her it was okay because, "There is one thing I've taught you that you haven't forgotten. You've learned to learn throughout your whole life." Those words were true when they were spoken in the late 1960s, and they are perhaps even truer today as our world, and its problems, increases in complexity. These words also capture the spirit of the next generation of standards and assessments.

As we emphasized in Chapter 2, "The only thing worth learning is learning how to learn, how to frame problems and pursue solutions." Fostering a lifelong love of learning in students is one of the greatest contributions a teacher can make; by embracing service learning, teachers can take this a step further by inspiring students to also become lifelong activists in their communities and problem-solvers. Seeing the positive contributions of one's actions in the local community and environment—and by extension, globally—makes these positive outcomes and the development of a lifelong dynamic mindset all the more likely.

CHAPTER 8

Service and Self-Renewal

Service Learning as a Means to Invigorate and Renew Teachers

Service learning leads to engaged students joyfully learning substantive content and significant strategies, making meaningful contributions to address real issues, and exulting in the ways that they are growing as individuals who are able to benefit themselves as well as others. Such outcomes are the reason why Angela Housley, Nancy Neely, and Libbie Hayden became teachers:

> *Angela:* When you see your students experience authentic learning and authentic engagement, that's pretty intoxicating and validating. That's why I became a teacher.
>
> *Nancy:* You know when you've hit that in your classroom. You see it in their faces. You know when you've engaged them. That's what we all look for; we *want* to engage our learners. We *want* them to be curious and excited and eager to come to class. We want them to know they are lifelong learners and problem-solvers. We're working for that spark.
>
> *Libbie:* Service learning brings about so much growth in students. They feel that they have done something for other people, and it makes them feel valuable in their world.

Similar hopes and dreams probably lead most teachers to this career and encourage us to remain in it. Service learning can be a vehicle for making such dreams into a continuous reality.

Thriving learning communities form the heart of effective service learning experiences. When looking back on her favorite teaching experiences, Whitney recognized that they occurred with inquiry and service learning projects because her students came together as a community doing significant work that involved them all. They were collectively invested in the project and able to have more in-depth discussions and build knowledge through their collective energy and the sense of accountability that they felt to the learning community. When the classroom is a community, it is a more engaging, joyful, and collaborative space to be for both students and teachers. Creating a problem-solving community helps foster a third space of transformation.

In his compelling book *Life in a Crowded Place*, Ralph Peterson (1992) offered powerful insights into why learning communities are important:

> the way human beings learn has nothing to do with being kept quiet. It has to do with our desire to make sense of our experience, to join with others, to become part of a community. It has to do with developing our expressive abilities and participating in everything that interests us, with being able to benefit from the insight and experience of others as we work at making the world take on meaning for ourselves, with living and learning in a place outfitted with opportunities to learn, a place where we can fumble and make mistakes without being scorned or laughed it. And it has to do with being responsible for our own learning. In short, it has to *mean* something to us. (p. 3)

One of the ways in which service learning provides a service to teachers is by supporting our work in cocreating learning communities with our students.

Our teaching, and that of the teachers with whom we work, is invigorated by students' input and by the work our students do with service learning in the context of inquiry framed by the already existing curriculum. We genuinely look forward to working with students who are engaged in such learning, to reading and responding to their work, and we find this model of teaching and learning significantly more engaging than other approaches to teaching. It maintains our passion for the profession, and it facilitates our growth as educators as we collaborate with students to engage with ourselves, one another, and the world.

It's useful to remember that we are teachers because we are committed to serving our students and their learning. We need to learn from our students—from the very beginning of any teaching/learning episode as well as throughout it—how to best teach them. We can be informed in our planning by engaging students in various entry points for service learning and inquiry projects: Observe and listen to students; ask students directly; and engage jointly with students in real research (Figure 8.1).

FORGING CONNECTION AND CREATING COMMUNITY

When students are collaborators, they are energized in ways that renew us as teachers. When students are engaged, many of the most salient problems of teaching are naturally solved, and we can concentrate on doing real work and achieving real learning. This learning is purposeful and relational and rooted in community.

First-grade teacher Shawntae Gardner finds service learning helpful because of how it helps her make curriculum meaningful. She explained, "Everything has this end goal; everything has this one big idea. Just like life, everything is interconnected, and I want it to feel that way in the classroom, too." Shawntae's words and experiences with service learning illustrate what Parker J. Palmer (1998) stated:

Figure 8.1. Three Approaches to Using Student Interest as the Entry Point for Service Learning

Approach		Guiding Questions
Listen to Students	From responding with interest when students are enthusiastic about something like the opportunity to raise a shark, to being incensed about human rights violations, to being an attentive listener to student conversations, teachers can identify potential topics. Remember that the underlying goal of inquiry is to connect students personally to the material of the curriculum and then connect what is learned back to the world in a way that it can be used.	What interests your students? What are topics you've (over)heard students discussing lately? Could any of their interests open up opportunities for service learning focused around inquiry into an existential/essential question? How can you involve kids in articulating those existential/essential questions and subquestions, and in identifying culminating service projects? When Angela Housley heard students complaining about the playground, she made rethinking how the playground was used an object of service learning.
Ask Students	Teachers can intentionally share dilemmas that pose possible topics for service learning with students to gauge student interest. Shari Griffin's trash in the hallways project would never have unfolded without student interest. Invite students to *be in* the conversation through essential questions such as: What is our proper relationship to the environment? How can we move toward becoming a zero-waste school?	What are some topics that you think your students might care about that might lend themselves to service learning projects? How can these topics be embedded in the existing curriculum or used to extend the existing curriculum? For example, while reading *To Kill a Mockingbird*, Sarah Veigel asked her students how they could become an Atticus, and how they could serve potential mockingbirds, helping them to find their voice and place in the community.
Student Research	Teachers can tell students that they will be asked to apply what they are learning in a unit as a kind of service. Students can then have the opportunity to engage in a service learning project and explain the parameters for a project. Then give students opportunities to work in teams to discuss potential topics and conduct initial research into the viability of the topics that interest them the most. Be aware: This approach can lead to multiple projects at one time if student interest is divided!	If you give students the opportunity to identify and vote on potential service learning projects, what will your parameters be? For example, do you want to make sure there is a local connection to the topic so community experts can serve as resources and potential guest speakers? Local topics allow teachers to conduct studies nearby and take advantage of local resources and support. Students can learn transferable concepts and strategies that can be applied globally..

Good teachers possess a capacity for connectedness. They are able to weave a complex web of connections among themselves, their subjects, and their students so that students can learn to weave a world for themselves. . . . The connections made by good teachers are not held in their methods but in their hearts—meaning *heart* in its ancient sense, as the place where intellect and emotion and spirit and will converge in the human self. (p. 11)

Inquiry that leads to service learning is a method of teaching that allows teachers to share their hearts with their students, and in the process, help children develop their own hearts while learning important skills and content in authentic contexts. Jeff called this teaching for love and wisdom, and it contributes to the passion and joy that animates "teaching and every interaction with the material, with individual students or the group. There is an implicit and sometimes an explicit cultivation of joy" (Wilhelm & Novak, 2011, p. 7).

Though students are our primary stakeholders and source of renewal, we have found that service learning creates natural partnerships with other teachers, with parents, and with the community that promote our work and renew us as teachers.

Connecting with Colleagues

Any time a teacher initiates a new form of curriculum and instruction it is, as Jeff likes to say, "doomed to some level of success." When we try new things we learn and grow, but there are inevitable challenges along the way. To navigate the process of experimenting with a new curricular approach, we recommend that colleagues join together and implement service learning as thinking partners and collaborators (see Figure 8.2). Meeting on a regular basis to share the progress of service learning projects and troubleshoot can help teachers refine their approach. Thinking partners can also offer constructive feedback on ideas, helping individual teachers see beyond their own perspective to plan better learning experiences for students. Peggy Jo Wilhelm did this for Jeff (as described in Chapter 2) by pushing him to ask deep, existential inquiry questions so that he was teaching for wisdom and use, for understanding and service in deep and meaningful ways that are about life and learning. We—Jeff, Whitney, and Sara—provide this kind of support for one another and for K–12 colleagues through our thinking partnerships, mentoring, and service learning support group.

In addition to having the capacity to help improve service learning projects, work as thinking partners provides rewarding collegial connections. When challenges arise and seem overwhelming, thinking partners serve as mentors who see possibilities and remind one another of the greater purpose of teaching with service learning. Positive collegial connections and support help teachers remain and thrive in the profession. Collegial connections among thinking partners Libbie Hayden, Angela Housley, and Nancy Neely are strong, although they all teach

Figure 8.2. Collaboration and Collegiality Through Thinking Partners

Step 1: Identify teachers in your school or district with whom you have a good rapport *and* who are interested in trying new pedagogy. Invite one or several to join you in a thinking partner collaboration.

Step 2: If this is your first time working together, establish ground rules for sharing and offering feedback. A shared commitment to principles like the following can help you create an effective and helpful partnership:

1. If presenting or sharing your work, ask for the kind of feedback that you want.
2. If responding, ask permission to provide feedback on a specific issue or element, even if this feedback has been asked for.
3. Frame feedback in positive, supportive, and encouraging ways.
4. If the presenter, listen to feedback with an open mind.
5. Frame feedback procedurally by describing what you see and the effect of these teaching moves or techniques on learners and learning.
6. Frame suggestions positively with "I wonder what would happen if. . . ."
7. Always remember that our students' success is at the heart of why we're collaborating.

You may also find it helpful to engage in a conversation about high-quality feedback before your first thinking partner meeting. You and your partners could review the following coaching comments; determine which ones are most helpful, concrete, and exhibit the dynamic mindset; and rephrase ones that are not.

1. I thought the lesson was just fine.
2. If I were doing the lesson, I would never have used that method.
3. The way you pay close attention to details, in particular the way you have all of the students engaged in some type of activity from the beginning of the lesson until the end, and how you move around monitoring and giving feedback to them all had the effect of helping all the students be engaged and involved and able to ask questions as needed.
4. Where does it say in the curriculum guide that kids in that class should write this type of composition?
5. This lesson could be used for your observation by the principal.
6. The way you immediately immersed students in an activity that you then reflected upon moved them directly into the lesson.
7. I think your energy level is fantastic and really engages the students and gets them enthused.

You can practice revising less effective comments into procedural feedback or causal statements.

Step 3: Engage in regular thinking partner meetings. When you're first getting started, it may be helpful to set regular meeting times (e.g., once a week for 30 minutes before school starts). Once you've established rapport, meetings will often happen spontaneously. For example, Nancy, Libbie, and Angela regularly find one another after school or even during a planning period for a quick check-in when a teaching dilemma or opportunity arises. Consider using the peer coaching protocol in step 2 above to provide structure for your time together.

Step 4: Enjoy the myriad results—from positive collegial connections to improved teaching and learning, thinking partnerships help us strengthen and renew our work.

different grades in the same school (5th, 4th, and 1st, respectively). These three teachers had supported one another in informal, serendipitous ways for several years before joining the BSWP service learning initiative, regularly eating lunch together and discussing teaching.

In the BSWP service learning initiative, we form more structured teams of thinking partners, with mentor teachers inducting participants into the use of inquiry to promote service learning. The mentors are teachers who have been successfully teaching with service learning and inquiry for several years, and they feel ready to guide and support other teachers in transforming their own classrooms and curriculum. Participants are usually pairs or triads from the same school, and the mentor may or may not be from that school. The mentor and participants schedule regular check-ins for one another, serving as "running buddies" who help each other stay on course. And we always share our work with both one another and the public at an annual Night of Inquiry event.

In addition to being transformative for participants, these kinds of collegial connections are uplifting for the mentors. Jeff's wife, Peggy Jo, has served as a mentor/thinking partner for several teachers in our initiatives, including Angela Housley. In Chapter 2, we described how Peggy Jo has a life-threatening illness. Despite having suffered 19 brain bleeds and being permanently disabled, Peggy Jo remains committed to children and teachers. She is able to go to schools, observe and coteach, and correspond and meet regularly with a few teachers who are implementing inquiry and service learning. She provides service by remaining involved as a teacher of teachers and kids in the ways that her condition and energy level allow, and she receives the service of staying involved in her passions and profession. She models how one can overcome challenges to stay involved in community life. She receives the energy of teachers and students who are doing significant work.

Connecting with Teacher Educators and Mentors

Another potential point of connection is with teacher educators at local universities or with teacher leaders in the school. In our service learning initiative, we regularly team experienced teachers with preservice teachers for a year-long student teaching experience in which they are actively supported as part of a larger group to create and implement inquiry and service learning curriculum.

Benefits of this approach include that teacher mentors and preservice teachers have a common project to work on together: creating and implementing an inquiry unit that integrates service learning. This meant that they had to collaborate and reflect together from well before the teaching experience and all the way through it. This project was an extended occasion for the mentor and student teacher to work together, share expertise and ideas, and collaborate in creating classroom culture together. Teacher preparation and K–12 pedagogy improved simultaneously.

The same could be true for teacher mentoring programs inside a school, where experienced teachers mentor new teachers into the profession and into new kinds of teaching, assessment processes, and so on. Given the new push for teacher evaluation that comes with implementation of the CCSS and the next generation of standards, this kind of mentoring could be hugely helpful to new as well as experienced teachers, since both provide a service to each other: experienced teachers inducting the new teachers into the profession, and the new teachers sharing their energy and the latest ideas and research from their recent university experiences.

Connecting with Parents

Parents are another site of resource and support, as they can reinforce and extend at home what students are learning and doing at school. First-grade teacher Sarah Bruskotter learned the importance of service learning when parent Sara Seely emailed her a heartfelt thanks and shared a picture (Figure 8.3) depicting the results of a successful family meeting to address the chronic problem her sons were having with being on time for the school bus.

Figure 8.3. Example of a Family Re-Enforcing Service Learning at Home

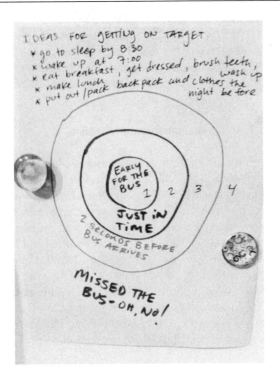

The first couple of weeks of the school year had been an uphill battle, with Sara struggling to motivate her sons to value the peace and tranquility of an unrushed morning. The situation was transformed after her 1st-grader Simon started to embrace the "getting on target" approach he was learning in school. "Getting on target" is part of a schoolwide language that teachers and students use as part of a process for encouraging students to meet learning outcomes. Students like Simon learn at a young age to self-monitor their progress and to be responsible for their success as learners.

Having shared language and expectations throughout the school fosters a sense of consistency as well as community. Communicating this language and these expectations to parents can get them to help support the work of the school *and* can help parents do similar work at home. Developing self-regulation, self-assessment skills, and projects with service to self as the outcome were at the heart of the 1st-grade curriculum at Simon's school. The language of "getting on target" made sense to Simon; the bull's eye was the ultimate, most rewarding goal, and it was hard to achieve. The rings around the bull's eye offered different levels of success, making it clear that Simon could still be successful even if the bull's eye wasn't entirely achievable yet.

Sara, who had also learned about getting on target at parent orientation, decided to apply this model to the "catching the school bus" issue that had been such a struggle. Having consistent language at school and home helped Simon be more successful in developing self-regulation skills. The community of Simon's classroom and school helped inform and strengthen the community at home.

For Sarah Bruskotter, the thank-you email from Sara offered more than words of gratitude; it illustrated that her teaching mattered and had an impact on Simon and his family. Sarah shared the getting on target example Sara Seely told her about with other parents as a way to encourage families to deepen their children's learning by giving them opportunities to apply their knowledge at home.

Anastasia Jenkins, whose 6th-grade daughter Asia attends an elementary school with a schoolwide emphasis on service learning, also believes her daughter's in-school learning experience has a positive impact on home life. Asia has 7 years of experience with the language of service learning—that's 7 formative years of her young life in which she has had meaningful opportunities to learn that we have an obligation to help others, to serve and better ourselves and our communities, or, as Anastasia succinctly put it, that "we're all in this together." It's a positive shift from Anastasia's own experience as a K–12 student. She reflected, "From a young age, Asia has learned about concepts I didn't even really think about until I was older." Asia's enthusiasm for in-school service projects comes home with her and has a trickle-out effect; as Anastasia explained, "It's made me consider what do I do outside of school to instill this ethic of caring!"

Anastasia purposefully reinforces the disposition Asia is developing at school through conversation and action at home. This sort of close school-home connection validates teachers' work, reinforces our in-school efforts, and provides the optimal learning experiences to help children like Asia develop into lifelong learners with the habits of mind to be active citizens. Creating classrooms that are caring places, and providing opportunities for parents to support us and serve as collaborators, strengthens the impact of our work.

EMPOWERING STUDENTS INVIGORATES TEACHERS

Teaching is hard work. Connecting with students, designing curriculum, implementing effective instruction, and providing meaningful and timely assessment of learning is more than enough to fill a day. The impossible-to-anticipate challenges that students will inevitably present, whether or not teachers are using service learning, can require a great deal of additional time, support, and attention from teachers. Although some problems will always require teachers to intervene, service learning can help students develop problem-solving skills that allow them to assume more responsibility for their actions and for the well-being of everyone in their classroom.

Elementary teachers know the importance of empowering children to become problem-solvers to avoid being bombarded with unhappy students due to conflicts. Our 4th-grade colleague Bridgette Downey was used to successfully facing this situation, but one year her usual approach to teaching students to manage conflicts fell short. The post-recess unhappiness seemed worse than previous years—at least six or more children were tearful, angry, and unable to focus on their schoolwork after recess each day. Bridgette started collecting data to try to understand the problem better, and soon realized that the same four girls were involved in every conflict each day, even though the other children involved might vary.

Bridgette also knew the four girls faced an array of challenges in their lives outside of school; helping them build their self-esteem and self-regulation abilities was essential. Bridgette invited the four girls to have lunch with her twice a week. The positive interaction time with their teacher, focused conversations about friendship, and gradual development of friendship with their peer group that had before been fraught with conflict was an empowering experience. Before long, the girls who had created daily conflict affecting the entire class were consciously striving toward becoming positive role models and friends.

The process provided service to Bridgette as a teacher, since instead of investing "stressful time" each day after recess mitigating conflict and re-creating a supportive classroom environment, Bridgette spent "positive time" with the girls, developing their self-esteem and social interaction skills. Although it was hard to carve out the time at lunch that might have otherwise been spent decompressing or planning, the time was worth it.

If Bridgette's story ended there, it would be enough, but the journey continued. As we have demonstrated with previous examples throughout this book, service spirals outward and often naturally leads to another form of service. Aware of the changes that had transformed them, the girls knew that other children often faced conflicts at recess. They decided to help educate others about friendship. Their lunch dates morphed into script writing and practice; the girls developed an informative skit about how to be a good friend. They performed the skit for younger students, transforming their service to self into service to school.

Children naturally want to share the results of their learning with others; with service learning, the product becomes authentic and useful. For Bridgette, providing a space for service to self did more than just release her from the unpleasant role of referee. The process of seeing students transform from children who were regularly involved in conflict to compassionate school leaders was invigorating because it allowed Bridgette to embrace the energizing and rejuvenating roles of collaborator and helpmate.

STUDENT FEEDBACK ENERGIZES TEACHERS

Service learning not only infuses a particular class with the positive energy of possibility, but also infuses energy into our teaching—both current and future. We've had the privilege of having some of the most excited and enlightened discussions with our students about disciplinary concepts and knowledge because service learning has facilitated more nuanced understandings and deeper learning. Student responses to their service learning experiences provide feedback that energizes and validates our work.

Whitney's students frequently indicate how a service learning project helped them connect the dots in ways they haven't always been able to do in their educational experiences. She is especially renewed when she reads student writing that genuinely engages her as a thinker and reader, making her momentarily forget that she is assessing a student's work because she finds herself revisiting a text or experience through the new lens that a student has provided. Whitney regularly points out how previous students' intellectual work is shaping a class discussion, activity, or assignment. Through service learning, her own commitment to teaching for love, wisdom, and democratic engagement is renewed.

In another example, our colleague Samantha Archibald Mora, a high school English, Spanish, and English language learner (ELL) teacher, received invigorating feedback from students involved in a service learning project she called Breaking Social Barriers. Samantha was concerned that many refugee students enrolled in her school's intensive ELL program had little access to native English speakers other than teachers and staff. The only time they interacted with mainstream students was during elective classes, which provided insufficient opportunities to practice their English with native speakers, learn social norms, and have a "normal" high school experience. Samantha also believed that U.S.-born students were missing authentic and engaging opportunities to learn about the world from their New American peers.

Breaking Social Barriers brought students in Samantha's advanced English class together with ELL students for a cultural exchange and ethnography project. The process enhanced student understanding and compassion, created space to form friendships, and led to impressive ethnographies; ELL students practiced academic English while advanced students moved toward deep cultural understandings and an appreciation of multiple perspectives and the challenges of the refugee experience, as well as mastery of the CCSS. Student reflections about the experience were phenomenally validating for Samantha. One native English speaker wrote:

> It is really important to do this next year!!!!! It will benefit ELL students and other students. It will help the ELL students feel more welcome and even make friendships that will last outside of Mrs. Mora's classroom. It will help everyone else because it will teach future students how the ELL kids are fun and really outgoing, and they will spread the word and make our school just a comfortable place for everybody. Maybe even someday the "racial cliques" will be gone!

Many of the ELL students had been nervous to be part of the class. On the last formal day of the exchange, one of the shyest refugee students made a thank-you speech to the entire class. She reflected on how the refugee students' impressions of the project had shifted:

> When we first heard about this project, some of us were scared and nervous. Others of us did not want to go to your classroom because we did not like the word *refugee* or *immigrant*. We did not want to go to a class of American students as a group of refugees. One of us even tried to go to another room and call home to say that she needed to go home because she was sick! This was all because of fear. When we began talking and found out that you do understand what refugee and immigrant means, that you didn't mean anything bad about us. When we started talking together, we think that we became friends. . . . We were excited to tell you about our cultures, especially about school, food, and how we are both different and the same. We also learned a lot about you, what you look like, what color you are, and how you act, and how you live. We found out that even though we are different colors, religions, and cultures, we are all humans. . . . From all of us in [the ELL class], we want to say thank you for everything you have done for us, and making us feel comfortable with ourselves. To Mrs. Mora, thank you for having this idea, and inviting us to your room. We . . . think you are COOL.

Samantha considers Breaking Social Barriers one of her best experiences as a teacher. High-quality service learning projects provide students with meaningful learning experiences that transform them into more thoughtful and knowledgeable citizens. Equally important is how teachers' hearts are renewed and how service learning projects provide a source of joy with positive feedback from students.

RENEWAL AND INVIGORATION IN A CLIMATE OF REFORM

Professional invigoration is essential to longevity as a teacher. As Livsey (1999) pointed out, "Teaching is a vocation that requires constant renewal of mind and heart and spirit—if we want to avoid burnout, take joy in our work, and grow in our service to students" (p. 5). Palmer (1998) described the necessity of attending to that renewal, given a social and political landscape that often finds teachers at fault for many things:

> Teaching and learning are critical to our individual and collective survival and to the quality of our lives. The pace of change has us snarled in complexities, confusions, and conflicts that will diminish, or do us in, if we do not enlarge our capacity to teach and to learn. At the same time, teacher-bashing has become a popular sport. Panic-stricken by the demands of our day, we need scapegoats for the problems we cannot solve and the sins we cannot bear.
>
> Teachers make an easy target, for they are such a common species and so powerless to strike back. We blame teachers for being unable to cure social ills that no one knows how to treat; we insist that they instantly adopt whatever "solution" has most recently been concocted by our national panacea machine; and in the process, we demoralize, even paralyze, the very teachers who could help us find our way. (p. 3)

The spirit of the myriad educational reforms that have swept the United States over the past quarter of a century has resulted in a climate of change and close scrutiny of teachers' work. These reforms have offered teachers many challenges. However, the current moment holds the potential for many positive possibilities—for teaching in ways that are supported by cognitive science and basic human needs, and for teaching in ways that offer proof positive of learning and of the value of that learning in the community that can be shared and celebrated in ways that promote teachers and learners and their substantive work. This kind of work demonstrates and celebrates teacher professionalism and student learning.

Although the teachers we work with have been challenged by the shifting landscape, they have responded bravely. Many have found their voices, taking action as citizens to try to improve the educational landscape in their school districts and state. They act as civic agents proactively aiming to (re)reform education, while continuing to grow as professional educators as they refine their approaches to teaching with inquiry-based approaches and service learning for the benefit of their students.

Service learning can help teachers find and assert our voices, in direct and implicit ways through active modeling and actual accomplishment, even when direct social action is not an option. For example, in Samantha Mora's school district, ELL students and native English speakers are rarely in the same classroom. Samantha's Breaking Social Barriers project provided the students with personally meaningful and academically rich opportunities for interaction. Lacking the power to change the policy itself, Samantha creatively addressed the separation in a way that enriched all students' lives, both those of traditional American students and recent refugees.

This is a major takeaway: Service learning allows teachers to meet the requirements outlined in the CCSS, and it is valuable in a way that transcends particular tests or standards in the ways it works toward higher purposes, as Samantha's project illustrates so beautifully. Service learning can provide teachers with a pathway to work through or around practices and policies that are not to our students' benefit, or that have not yet been fully actualized for their benefit.

Jeff and Angela provide another example, as they are also activist teachers who work toward more choice around canonical lists of reading materials. In addition to required readings, they have purposefully created free-choice reading programs and small-group literature circles and book clubs as ways of including popular children's and young adult books in the classroom. They purposefully use books that students love (e.g., *Harry Potter, The Hunger Games*) to help students engage as readers and to promote the standards in the CCSS. Often, these are books that many educators, administrators, or even parents don't see as "schoolish" enough, but celebrating this kind of reading in tangential ways has been hugely successful.

Jeff and Angela focus their efforts on celebrating what students do with books instead of focusing on the books themselves. Instead of insisting on textual complexity, they focus on interpretive content and complexity, celebrating and encouraging students to be avid readers and guiding them to interpret and make complex analyses of the content. Jeff's commitment to promoting engaged readership led him, Michael Smith, and Sharon Fransen (2014) to write a book-length guide for teachers to help them take on this approach: *Reading Unbound: Why Kids Need to Read What They Want—and Why We Should Let Them.*

IT'S YOUR TURN

Throughout this book we have provided specific examples of the kinds of inspiring teaching and learning that occur when inquiry and service learning are combined. The next step is yours. Angela offered the advice, "Be practical and start small. Students have to write and read *something*. They may as well write or create something that's usable to themselves and to someone else." To begin your journey into service learning, you might start by identifying a unit that you teach that you want to revise anyway.

Angela had this to say about how teacher and student expertise combine to create powerful service learning and inquiry:

Our expertise is that we know the skills kids need to do a project and how to develop the skills and knowledge they need in the Common Core. That's what they don't know. Their skill is that they know what they love to do. In that way it is a shared endeavor—we don't need to control—we just need to know what *they need* to know—and then how to help them learn to know and do these things, so they can do what they are already excited to do.

Regardless of the grade level you teach, service learning and inquiry can provide opportunities for unparalleled student growth and accomplishment.

The CCSS and all the next generation standards and assessments focus on higher-order thinking and reading, composing, speaking, and listening as pathways to disciplinary work. Both inquiry and service learning cultivate, require, and reward literacy. Through the pursuit of service learning and inquiry projects, students develop and apply literacy and disciplinary knowledge, see firsthand the real-world implications and uses of such learning, learn to think in more connected ways, and simultaneously acquire the literacies that are essential for creating a culture of civic engagement. The next step toward engagement and joy in your classroom and the next step toward a more just and democratic world filled with activist citizens begins with you and your students.

How will you begin?

Afterword: *The* Change

Everything has changed...except the way we think
—Albert Einstein

Produce great Persons. The rest follows.
—Walt Whitman

You have just read a book about the *true* "common core" of education. Amid all the talk of "high educational standards," the public, and many educators, have forgotten that the most important high standards to have are moral ones. This book is a powerful reminder of that, and also a powerful reminder that when we assist young people in their yearning to be a part of something larger than just themselves they tend as well to become far more intelligent and engaged than when we merely pander mindlessly to their narrow self-interest, as so much education has always done. Education *is not* educative in the final sense, unless it *draws us out* of our narrow self-interest and *gives us* interest in things larger than ourselves. But, particularly in this age of imminent ecological crisis, our species appears to be doomed unless we can rapidly develop ecological *consciousness* in the upcoming generations—and this entails far more than consciousness about environmental issues. It is *transactional* consciousness of how all beings are meaningfully and existentially wrapped up in one another, and of how human beings become human only when they are actively and meaningfully enwrapped in a world they have come to care about. This book, more than any other I know, shows both the classroom hows and the worldly whys to bring that consciousness about.

A few years ago, Jeff and I wrote a book called *Teaching Literacy for Love and Wisdom: Being the Book and Being the Change* (Wilhelm & Novak, 2011) in which we teased out the intimate ecology of existential inquiry. Drawing on ideas first framed in Jeff's earlier "*You Gotta BE the Book*," we focused there mostly on the processes of existential inquiry in literary reading—which, in the terms of *activist learning*, is an especially important form of "self-service." It is important because, like all art, it is a special kind of gift, a "third space" of experience in which we live for a time enwrapped in the consciousness of another as well as our own. The central purpose of art, though, is to prepare us to *live* in this "third space": to seek transactional, ecological consciousness in life; to seek to live in reality poetically;

to seek to make in actual, responsible moral life the kinds of intimate connections that come naturally in the responsive flow of art.

So I see the book you are now holding in your hands as being very much a companion piece to the book Jeff and I wrote together. It is about how to *artfully* accomplish, and assist students in artfully accomplishing, in everyday classroom circumstances, "*the* change" that we all want and need to see *in the world*—the change that Socrates, Buddha, Confucius, and Jesus all longed to see, and that we now most likely *need* to see for our very survival—the change from a society dominated self-defeatingly by self-interest narrowly conceived to a society that regularly cultivates and enacts ecological, transactional consciousness, creating artfully realized "third space," not just in the imagination, but everywhere. Peter Block (1996), in *Stewardship: Choosing Service over Self-Interest* and Riane Eisler (2007), in *The REAL Wealth of Nations: Creating a Caring Economics* both show how creating this change can actually create both a more prosperous and a more sustainable economy than the one we now have. And Mark Hansen (2012), in *Hardwiring Happiness*, shows how the experience of connection, if methodically cultivated, produces a permanent change in the neuronal structure of our brains—it artfully creates *happiness itself*, delusory images of which so many of us, and so much of our education system, blindly pursue. But despite all these palpable incentives for this change to ecological, transactional consciousness to occur, it is hardly a foregone conclusion that we will be able to accomplish it in time to avoid unprecedented disaster.

In 2008, "the change we need" was a political slogan in a presidential campaign. But this book is about the *real* change we need—a change in consciousness, in personhood, in education, and, ultimately, in democratic moral life. After reading it, you now know a lot more about how to be the change. Now go. Be it! And help your students be it! For the change is up to all of us.

Bruce Novak

REFERENCES

Block, P. (1996). *Stewardship: Choosing service over self-interest.* San Francisco, CA: Berrett-Koehler.

Eisler, R. (2007). *The REAL wealth of nations: Creating a caring economics.* San Francisco, CA: Berrett-Koehler.

Hansen, R. (2012). *Hardwiring happiness: The new brain science of contentment, calm, and confidence.* New York, NY: Harmony.

Wilhelm, J. D., & Novak, B. (2011). *Teaching literacy for love and wisdom: Being the BOOK and being the CHANGE.* New York, NY: Teachers College Press.

References

Allen, R. (2003). The democratic aims of service learning. *Educational Leadership, 60*(6), 51–55.

Barcott, B. (2008). *The last flight of the scarlet macaw.* New York, NY: Random House.

Bird Exploration. (2012). Anser charter school. Available at www.ansercharter-school.org/classrooms/kindergarten/

Bloom, B. (1976). *Human characteristics and school learning.* New York, NY: McGraw-Hill.

Boas, E., Wilhelm, F. & Wilhelm, J. (2014). *Food.* Toronto: Scholastic Canada.

Bringle, R. G., & Hatcher, J. A. (2003). Reflection in service learning: Making meaning of experience. In *Introduction to service-learning toolkit: Readings and resources for faculty.* (2nd ed., pp. 83–89). Providence, RI: Campus Compact.

Brint, S., Contreras, M. F., & Matthews, M. (2001). Socialization messages in primary schools: An organizational analysis. *Sociology of Education, 74*(3), 157–180.

Brown, J., Collins, A., & Duguid, P. (1989). Situated cognition and the culture of learning. *Educational Researcher 18*(1), 32–42.

Burke, K. (1973). *The philosophy of literary form* (3rd ed.). Berkeley, CA: University of California Press.

Christie, E. M., Montgomery, S. E., & Staudt, J. (2012). Little by little: Global citizenship inspired through local action. *Social Studies and the Young Learner, 25*(2), 8–11.

Cushman, E. (1996). The rhetorician as an agent of social change. *College Composition and Communication, 47*(1), 7–28.

D'Aluisio, F., & Menzel, P. (2008). *What the world eats.* Berkeley, CA: Tricycle Press.

DeStigter, T. (2001). *Reflections of a citizen teacher: Literacy, democracy, and the forgotten students of Addison High.* Urbana, IL: National Council of Teachers of English.

Dewey, J. (1916). *Democracy and education.* New York, NY: The Free Press.

Dewey, J., & Bentley, A. (1949). *Knowing and the known.* Boston, MA: Beacon Press.

Do'anay, A. (2012). A curriculum framework for active democratic citizenship education. In M. Print & D. Lange (Eds.), *Schools, curriculum and civic education for building democratic citizens* (pp. 19–39). Rotterdam, Netherlands: Sense Publishers.

Doidge, N. (2007). *The brain that changes itself.* New York, NY: Penguin.

Dweck, C. (2006). *Mindset: The new psychology of success.* New York, NY: Random House.

Eiseley, L. C. (1978). *The star thrower.* New York, NY: Times Books.

Elbow, P. (1983). Embracing contraries in the teaching process. *College English, 45*(4), 327–339.

Elbow, P. (1998). *Writing without teachers.* New York, NY: Oxford University Press.

Flower, L. (2000). The rival hypothesis stance and the practice of inquiry. In L. Flower, E. Long, & L. Higgins (Eds.), *Learning to rival: A literate practice for intercultural inquiry* (pp. 27–48). Mahwah, NJ: Lawrence Erlbaum Associates.

Fry, S. W. (2012). From charity to solidarity. *Kappan, 93*(8), 76–77.

Fry, S. W., Griffin, S., & Kirshner, J. (2012). Global citizenship: Teachers and students in Belize and the U.S. take action together. *Social Studies and the Young Learner, 25*(2), 23–27.

Gee, J. P. (1999). *An introduction to discourse analysis: Theory and method.* New York, NY: Routledge.

Glass, I. (Producer). (1996, June 21.) The cruelty of children [Episode 27.] *This American Life Podcast.* Available at www.thisamericanlife.org

Goodlad, J. I. (2000). Education and democracy: Advancing the agenda. *The Phi Delta Kappan, 82*(1), 86–89.

Hillocks, G. (1983). *Research on written composition.* Urbana, IL: National Council of Teachers of English.

Hillocks, G. (1995). *Teaching writing as reflective practice.* New York, NY: Teachers College Press.

hooks, b. (1994). *Teaching to transgress: Education as the practice of freedom.* New York, NY: Routledge.

Institute for Intercultural Studies. (1999–2009). Frequently asked questions. Available at www.interculturalstudies.org/faq.html

Johnson, R. A. (1986). *Inner work: Using dreams and active imagination for personal growth.* New York, NY: HarperCollins Publishers.

Johnston, P. H. (2004). *Choice words.* Portland, ME: Stenhouse Publishers.

Johnston, P. H. (2012). *Opening minds: Using language to change lives.* Portland, ME: Stenhouse Publishers.

Kahne, J., & Middaugh, E. (2008) Democracy for some: The civic opportunity gap in high school. *CIRCLE Working Paper 59.* Available at www.civicsurvey.org/democracy_some_circle.pdf

Kaye, C. B. (2010). *The complete guide to service learning: Proven, practical ways to engage students in civic responsibility, academic curriculum, & social action* (Revised & updated ed.). Minneapolis, MN: Free Spirit Publishing.

Kessler, R. (2000). *The soul of education: Helping students find connection, compassion and character at school.* Alexandria, VA: ASCD.

Langer, J. A. (2001). Beating the odds: Teaching middle and high school students to read and write well. *American Educational Research Journal, 38*(4), 837–880.

Lave, J., & Wenger, E. (1991). *Situated learning: Legitimate peripheral participation.* New York, NY: Cambridge University Press.

Livsey, R. C. (1999). *The courage to teach: A guide for reflection and renewal.* San Francisco, CA: Jossey-Bass.

Moje, E. B, Ciechanowski, K. M., Kramer, K., Ellis, L., Carillo, R., & Collazo, T. (2004). Working toward third space in content area literacy: An examination of everyday funds of knowledge and discourse. *Reading Research Quarterly, 39*(1), 38–71.

Morton, K. (2010). The irony of service: charity, project, and social change in service-learning. In T. Deans, B. Roswell, & A. J. Wurr (Eds.), *Writing and community engagement: A critical sourcebook* (pp. 117–137). Boston, MA: Bedford/St. Martin's.

Moss, M. (2013). *Salt, sugar, fat.* New York, NY: Random House.

Nagel, P., & Beauboeuf, D. (2012). Yellow ducks overboard! A lesson in geography and world citizenship. *Social Studies and the Young Learner, 25*(2), 5–7.

National Council for the Social Studies (NCSS). (2010). *National Curriculum Standards for Social Studies: A framework for teaching, learning, and assessment.* Silver Spring, MD: NCSS.

Newman, F., & Associates. (1996). *Authentic achievement: Restructuring of schools for intellectual equality.* San Francisco, CA: Jossey-Bass.

Newman, F., & Wehlage, G. (1995). *Successful school restructuring: A report to the public and educators by the center on organization and restructuring of schools.* Madison, WI: Board of Regents of the University of Wisconsin System and Document Service, Wisconsin Center for Education Research.

Nieto, S. (2003). *What keeps teachers going?* (3rd ed.). New York, NY: Teachers College Press.

O'Reilly, M. (1998). *Radical presence: Teaching as contemplative practice.* Portsmouth, NH: Boynton/Cook.

Paley, V. G. (1993). *You can't say you can't play.* Cambridge, MA: Harvard Education.

Palmer, P. J. (1998). *The courage to teach: exploring the inner landscape of a teacher's life.* (11th ed.) San Francisco, CA: Jossey-Bass.

Peck, W. C., Flower, L., & Higgins, L. (1995). Community literacy. *College Composition and Communication, 46*(2), 199–222.

Perkins, D. N. (1986). *Knowledge as design.* Mahwah, NJ: Lawrence Erlbaum Associates.

Peterson, R. (1992). *Life in a crowded place.* Portsmouth, NH: Heinemann.

Ramsey, R. D. (2008). *DON'T teach the canaries NOT to sing: Creating a school culture that boosts achievement.* Thousand Oaks, CA: Corwin Press.

Rogoff, B., Matusov, E., & White, C. (1996). Models of teaching and learning: Participation in a community of learners. In D. R. Olsen & N. Torrance (Eds.), *The handbook of education and human development* (pp. 388–414). Cambridge, MA: Blackwell Publishers.

Salvatori, M. R. (2000). Difficulty: the great educational divide. In P. Hutchings (Ed.), *Opening lines: Approaches to the scholarship of teaching and learning* (pp. 81–93). Menlo Park, CA: The Carnegie Foundation for the Advancement of Teaching.

Sen, R. (2003). *Stir it up: Lessons in community organizing and advocacy.* San Francisco, CA: Jossey-Bass.

Shenk, D. (2010). *The genius in all of us: Why everything you've been told about genetics, talent, and intelligence is wrong.* New York, NY: Doubleday.

Shulman, L. (1986). Those who understand: Knowledge growth in teaching. *Educational Researcher, 15*(2), 4–14.

Smith, M. W., Appleman, D., & Wilhelm, J. D. (2014). *Uncommon core: Where the authors of standards go wrong about instruction—and how you can get it right.* Thousand Oaks, CA: Corwin.

Smith, M. W., & Wilhelm, J. D. (2002). *Reading don't fix no Chevys: Literacy in the lives of young men.* Portsmouth, NH: Heinemann.

Smith, M. W., & Wilhelm, J. D. (2006). *Going with the flow: How to engage boys (and girls) in their literacy learning.* Portsmouth, NH: Heinemann.

Smith, M. W., & Wilhelm, J. D. (2010). *Fresh takes on teaching literary elements: How to teach what really matters about character, setting, point of view, and theme.* New York, NY: Scholastic.

Smith, M. W., Wilhelm, J. D., & Fredricksen, J. E. (2013). *Oh yeah? Putting argument to work both in school and out.* Portsmouth, NH: Heinemann.

Tharp, R., & Gallimore, R. (1990). *Rousing minds to life: Teaching, learning, and schooling in social context.* Cambridge, UK: Cambridge University Press.

Vygotsky, L. (1962). *Thought and language.* Cambridge, MA: MIT Press.

Vygotsky, L. (1978). *Mind in society: The development of higher psychological processes.* Cambridge, MA: Harvard University Press.

Walker, A. (1998). *Anything we love can be saved: A writer's activism.* New York, NY: The Ballantine Publishing Group.

Wiggins, G., & McTighe, J. (2005). *Understanding by design.* Alexandria, VA: Association for Supervision and Curriculum Development.

Wilhelm, J. D. (2007). *Engaging readers and writers with inquiry.* New York, NY: Scholastic.

Wilhelm, J. D. (Ed.). (2008a). Next Steps in the Journey: Teaching with "Urgency:" A Call for Immediate Actions: A Call to Action. *Voices from the Middle, 16*(2), 54–57.

Wilhelm, J. D. (2008b). *You gotta be the book: Teaching engaged and reflective reading with adolescents* (2nd ed.). New York, NY: Teachers College Press.

Wilhelm, J. D. (2010). Wisdom and third space. *Voices from the Middle, 18*(2), 55–58.

Wilhelm, J. D. (2012a). *Deepening comprehension with action strategies: role plays, text-structure tableaux, talking statues, and other enactment techniques that engage students with text* [includes Stategies in Action on DVD]. New York, NY: Scholastic Teaching Resources.

Wilhelm, J. D. (2012b). *Enriching comprehension with visualization strategies: text elements and ideas to build comprehension, encourage reflective reading, and represent understanding* [includes Stategies in Action on DVD]. New York, NY: Scholastic Teaching Resources.

Wilhelm, J. D. (2012c). *Improving comprehension with think aloud strategies: Modeling what good readers do.* (2nd ed.). New York, NY: Scholastic Teaching Resources.

Wilhelm, J. D., Baker, T., & Dube, J. (2001). *Strategic reading.* Portsmouth, NH: Heinemann.

Wilhelm, J. D., & Novak, B. (2011). *Teaching literacy for love and wisdom: Being the BOOK and being the CHANGE.* New York, NY: Teachers College Press.

Wilhelm, J. D., Smith, M. W., Fransen, S. (2014). *Reading unbound: Why kids choose what they read and why we should let them.* New York, NY: Scholastic.

Wilhelm, J. D., Smith, M. W., & Fredricksen, J. E. (2013). *Get it done! Writing and analyzing informational texts to make things happen.* Portsmouth, NH: Heinemann.

Wilhelm, J. D., Wilhelm, P. J., & Boas, E. (2008). *Inquiring minds learn to read and write.* Ontario, Canada: Rubicon Publishing.

Winnicott, D. W. (1953). *Playing and reality.* London, UK: Tavistock Publications.

Index

An "f" following a page number refers to a figure.

About the Authors

Jeffrey D. Wilhelm is currently distinguished professor of English Education at Boise State University and regularly teaches middle and high school students. He is the founding director of the Maine Writing Project and the Boise State Writing Project, and author of 32 texts about literacy teaching and learning. He is the recipient of the two top research awards in English Education: the NCTE Promising Research Award for *You Gotta BE the Book* and the Russell Award for Distinguished Research for *Reading Don't Fix No Chevys*.

Whitney Douglas is an assistant professor of English at Boise State University, where she teaches classes in writing, rhetoric, and gender studies. Whitney wholeheartedly believes in her students' creative capacity to change the world for the better, and loves being inspired by them semester after semester.

Sara W. Fry is an associate professor of education at Boise State University, where she enjoys helping students recognize and develop their potential as activist, participatory citizens. As a member of the Belize Education Project, Sara is committed to empowering youth to improve their futures through literacy and education. Prior to her university career, Sara taught middle school social studies and language arts in Colorado and Trinidad and Tobago, and a big part of her heart is still in the middle.